Secrets to a Successful Commercial Software (COTS) Implementation

Secrets to a Successful Commercial Software (COTS) Implementation

Nick Berg

PMP, Program manager

iUniverse, Inc.
New York Lincoln Shanghai

Secrets to a Successful Commercial Software (COTS) Implementation

Copyright © 2008 by Nick Berg

iUniverse books may be ordered through booksellers or by contacting:

iUniverse
2021 Pine Lake Road, Suite 100
Lincoln, NE 68512
www.iuniverse.com
1-800-Authors (1-800-288-4677)

ISBN: 978-0-595-44433-5 (pbk)
ISBN: 978-0-595-68950-7 (cloth)
ISBN: 978-0-595-88760-6 (ebk)

Printed in the United States of America

To my beautiful wife, Sabrina. Without her support, this book would not have been possible.

Contents

Chapter One

Buy vs. Build

Introduction

The primary purpose of this book is to provide a good understanding on how commercial off-the-shelf (COTS) software should be implemented. This information should enable the reader to identify either new processes or modifications to existing processes in order to realize the benefits of COTS and an iterative process. Success absolutely depends on good project management processes that are refined over time. Expecting success by using traditional business practices, as many have learned, is a rash notion.

Building solutions based on preexisting COTS packages are different from typical green-field development. Numerous projects have unsuccessfully tried to integrate preexisting COTS packages by defining the requirements, formulating architecture to meet those requirements, and then trying to fit COTS packages into that architecture. The unique characteristics of COTS packages introduce dynamics and specific constraints that must be accommodated. Projects that build solutions based on COTS packages require dedicated guidance.

I will introduce a unique process for COTS development, a process that configures several processes including IBM Rational Unified Process (RUP), Extreme Programming (XP), and several other Agile development methodologies that addresses the needs of the readers who demand process guidance in their projects in order to evaluate, recommend, acquire, install, configure, field, and evolve solutions based on COTS packages. However, we will first introduce some best practice processes for COTS projects. Then we will define architecture process within the COTS environment. Finally, we will walk through each project phase of a COTS-based project by introducing the objectives, road map, roles, activities, artifacts, and milestone of the phase.

In today's world, most global companies face enormous challenges in dealing with a budget climate characterized by inflexibility when wrenching changes are required. Finding reasonable ways of saving money is essential. There are several possibilities, but most involve hard choices. Taking advantage of COTS products, for example, SAP, Seibel, and PeopleSoft, seems like a logical way to achieve significant cost savings with very little sacrifice. In addition, there are often other potential benefits including faster deployment time, improved quality and reliability, reduced development risk, and an already established support system.

However, in those organizations that have deployed COTS, only a few are realizing significant benefits. Based on research that Gartner completed in 2005, most organizations are struggling with its complexity. A few have failed miserably. The complexities are numerous and less than obvious. Arguably, the largest difficulty is inflexible end user requirements. The maximum utilization of COTS products demands flexible requirements from the outset. Organizations must interact with potential bidders before the statement of work and request for proposal (RFP) are established. A balance must be achieved between desired performance and what can be reasonably attained by integrating available and projected commercial products. During system development, trade studies should be conducted to further refine the balance among performance specifications, procedures, total ownership cost, and extent of COTS product utilization. Organizations must require continuous performance trades to maximize the use of COTS products.

Rigid requirements may result in relatively few suitable COTS products. Demanding the maximum use of COTS products while constraining requirements flexibility is a recipe for disaster. Something must give. The customer must be willing to accept the 80 percent solution role. That is, in the initial phase of the project, only 80 percent of the functionality will be available. If not, the organizations cannot count on the much-touted benefits of COTS. Inadequate consideration of COTS product volatility, deriving from the broad scale of COTS development and, particularly, in software, is another common snare that many experience. Integrating forty or fifty COTS software packages, each on an asynchronous eighteen-month upgrade cycle, is a challenge. A successful integration effort must deal with a constant state of flux.

In total, programs often experience several obstacles. But most could be avoided or mitigated if appropriate processes or procedures were in place that people understood and followed. Requirements must flow into an architecture that can truly exploit the advantages of COTS. Implementations must shift from "design and build" unique products to "buy and integrate" standard products. Business users as well as the IT department cope with a COTS development environment that has a very steep learning curve. Those who seem to do it well have been at it for many years. They freely admit they have made every mistake imaginable along the way. Unfortunately, others cannot imagine the mistakes they are about to make.

For both integrator and company personnel, the cultural differences and the mind-set of project cycles between a traditional custom company spec and a COTS-intensive environment are enormous. COTS demands new skills, knowledge, and abilities. The traditional skills, including gathering requirements and matching them to functions that are acquired over many years, do not provide an adequate understanding to address the additional complications in selecting, specifying, buying, and using commercial products for applications. Roles and responsibilities change dramatically. Hence, there is a need for an adequate cultural change management plan, which we will discuss later.

As shown in the following figure, processes are radically different. The ramifications of these shifts are enormous. For decades, company personnel have been conducting business a particular way. Now we are being asked to do it in an entirely different fashion. Many feel insecure about their jobs and a loss of control.

Traditional Approach vs. COTS Approach

Actually, this section could have been renamed "Waterfall Development vs. Iterative Development."

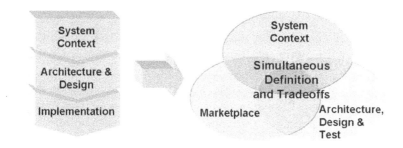

Figure 1. Fundamental development shift.

I will later describe the process on how the shift in methodologies happens. In most organizations, the operational community traditionally sets requirements, and the development community comes up with alternative concepts for meeting those requirements. COTS products are designed to meet the desires of the mass market. It is unlikely that the supplier of a COTS product will offer a modified version for a single, low-volume customer. Hence, if operational requirements are viewed as not negotiable and the suppliers are unwilling to modify their COTS products to meet unique needs, then the probability of finding an exact match between requirement and COTS product is diminished.

Often, for large companies, the solution to this dilemma has been to purchase the data rights to the supplier's source code. This assumes the rights are for sale. Else, the company paid and modified the COTS product itself. Although this approach can avoid the writing of some code, it voids the warranty on the COTS product and renders it no longer as COTS. The advantages of maintenance support and evolutionary upgrades are lost.

Companies that were successful in incorporating COTS products could trade off requirements with the operational and development communities in order to achieve a best value solution. Rigid requirements or an overly specific requirement deny the use of COTS products that could offer acceptable performance at lower total cost of ownership. In other words, it is better to adapt the requirements to the COTS product than the COTS product to the requirements. If field operators and program managers are unwilling or unable to do this, then they should not use COTS.

Potential Benefits

The incorporation of COTS products into organizations offers anticipated advantages, for example, initial price, reliability, availability, and support. This raises expectations for cost and schedule savings. When COTS products are incorporated into commercial systems, the following benefits are possible:

- **Lower cost:** If a commercial product, hardware or software, in widespread use can be found that provides a function needed in a new system or system upgrade, then developmental costs, for example, configurations and coding, which would generally be more expensive than the commercial product, can be avoided. Furthermore, if a company can rely on the commercial product vendor to maintain the product during its lifetime, support costs can potentially be reduced as well.

- **Faster deployment:** Because the commercial product is already available, custom development, which would generally take longer than integrating the commercial product, can be avoided.

- **Improved quality and reliability:** Because the commercial product is in widespread use, defects are likely to have been already identified and eliminated.

- **Leverage fast-paced commercial product evolution:** Due to competitive market pressures, the vendor of the commercial product will periodically offer improved versions of the product. These improved versions are available for incorporation into the system, resulting in potential system improvements.

- **Reduced development risk:** Because the commercial product is market-proven, the risk of providing its intended function in the system is mitigated.

- **Support system in place:** Because the vendor is already providing support of the commercial product, the system operators do not need to create their own support infrastructure.

- **Upgrades provided:** Because the vendor will offer improved versions of the product periodically, the cost of developing an upgrade to that function of the system can potentially be avoided.

- **More stable industrial base:** Because the supplier depends on a large commercial market, not solely on small-volume business, for survival, the supplier is more likely to remain in business.

- **Decreased reliance on sole providers:** The large market for a successful commercial product attracts competitors, creating alternate sources.

- **Facilitates innovation from small businesses/academia:** Intense competition in the commercial marketplace causes suppliers to actively seek technology that will differentiate their product from the others.

Potential Disadvantages

Commercial software has disadvantages as well. License fees are just one of them. For example, disadvantages are the possible limits of fitting the software to your requirements, its ability to integrate with your environment, and its ability to mature and develop with additional features. Because of its canned functions and features, a large amount of training may be required to accomplish end user processes.

- **Inappropriate application:** In many applications, COTS products are inappropriate. For example, commercial software should not be utilized where absolute trust in the software is essential, for example, controlling of nuclear weapons. Of particular concern for such applications is an embedded Trojan horse or trap door. Often, the functionality of the COTS product is not a good fit with the functional needs of the system. More time may be consumed to adapt the product than developing it from scratch.

- **Inadequate product volatility consideration:** The vendor must also have a proven methodology for coping with the frequent, asynchronous revisions to COTS products. New versions of a COTS software package may appear as frequently as every eighteen months. After three or four upgrades, the software vendor may choose to no longer maintain the earlier version incorporated in your system. Indeed, the obsolescence of a COTS product will occur even in the design stage, making it necessary for the initial production item to be different from the prototype. The vendor must have a program management process that accommodates this fact of life. This process would include an open system architecture that allows plug and play of replacement objects and an iterative development approach that plans for cyclic repetition of design, development, and test to create sequential versions of the system, devoid of obsolescence. Several of these cycles will be occurring simultaneously, albeit in different phases. The contractor must predict the change cycle for each embedded COTS product and plan for regular refresh of the system throughout the design, development, production, and sustainment phases of the program.

- **Lack of thorough COTS product evaluation:** The suitability of a particular COTS product must be evaluated on the basis of its total cost of ownership (TCO) as well as a set of performance specifications. These specifications will address the manner in which the COTS product must perform in order to satisfy a particular function in the system being procured. Failure to thoroughly test the COTS product to such a performance specification may result in surprising disappointments later.

Design and Build	Buy and Integrate (COTS)
Requirements-driven	Commercial market-driven
Specification-constrained	Trade-off-oriented
Rigid requirements	Flexible requirements
Unique architecture	Open system architecture
Owner controls product evolution	Market drives product evolution
Stable design	Constant changes
Ignores product evolution	Designed for evolution (technology refresh)
Recurring cost emphasis	Total ownership cost emphasis
Make custom hardware	Buy from catalog
Develop software	License software
Unplanned obsolescence	Managed obsolescence
Waterfall-style development	Spiral development
Customer standards	Widely accepted commercial standards

Table 1. Build vs. buy.

Summary

The cultural impact on an organization facing this decision is profound. Successfully fielding a COTS-based system and realizing the anticipated benefits is very difficult to do. Often, its complexity is underestimated. Like many management edicts, the devil is in the detail. And this is a particularly nasty devil.

As many have been led to believe, COTS is not a cure-all. Expecting major benefits, for example, lower costs and shorter development times without a major change in the way work is accomplished, is a risky notion. Every aspect of acquisition planning, system engineering processes, test planning, and so forth must be explicitly crafted to account for COTS issues.

Ideally, the organization's mentality ought to be "how we can do it" as opposed to "why we cannot." But not every new requirement can realistically be addressed with a COTS-based solution. The applications must be chosen carefully. The degree of implementation will depend on the specific application. Arbitrary mandates are dangerous. Company leadership and executive management needs to drive the insertion of COTS products. Else, the system will revert back to the old ways. But leadership needs to be mindful of the obstacles. If the business experts and the system implementation consultants say it is impractical, then listen. Attempting a COTS-based solution where it is entirely inappropriate will end in failure.

COTS is inevitable. Competitive pressures will eventually push most companies to change their ways and adopt good COTS practices. It will be virtually impossible to successfully compete with a traditional custom design approach.

Chapter Two

Waterfall vs. Iterative Process

The Waterfall Process

Waterfall development, or systems development life cycle model (SDLC), is an approach to software development that breaks a project into finite phases. Each phase is performed in order; each depends on the completion of preceding phases. At one point, it was believed that software development had a lot in common with engineering processes. Waterfall was once touted as a way to make software development cost-effective.

If coding began before the design was approved, some coding effort would probably be wasted. In practice, the construction mentality inherent in the waterfall process has led to some spectacular COTS implementation failures. For example, one company invested almost $20 million in an Enterprise Resource Planning (ERP) system using the waterfall process. The project was locked in the requirements phase for more than two years

Under the waterfall development method, each portion of work is evaluated separately. Different teams often perform each portion. There are various schools of thought about what the actual phases should be, but the progression always relies on heavy, up-front planning. A common breakdown of the waterfall development process includes:

1	Requirements	Evaluate the problem	<ul><li>Birth of the concept</li><li>Identify deficiencies with existing solutions</li><li>Gather information</li></ul>

2	Design	Propose a solution	• Present a detailed description of the solution, including pros and cons and the problems the software will address • Finalize timelines, budgets, work breakdown structures, and other supporting documentation • Most importantly, identify and analyze requirements
3	Build	Develop the code	• Use the blueprints created in previous phases to write, debug, and unit test the code • Integrate the code and test portions of the system • Test the entire system **Note:** This cycle is incomplete until all tests have passed.
4	Test	Test the system	• System test the developed code • Complete user acceptance testing
5	Deployment	Deploy and use the system	• Roll out the resulting functionality • Provide training and documentation to users as needed

Table 2. Common breakdown of the waterfall development process.

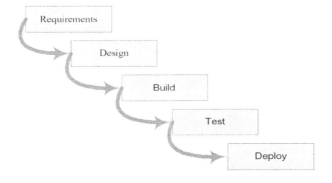

Figure 2. Waterfall process.

Waterfall Model Benefits

Benefits of the waterfall model include the following:

- The waterfall model has been around for a long time.
- Many people are familiar with the waterfall model.
- The waterfall model is very easy to understand.
- The waterfall model works very well for small software development projects.

Waterfall Model Weaknesses

While the waterfall model is easy to understand, it does have some weaknesses, especially in the context of COTS and configuration.

- COTS vendors do change features, but these are in response to the overall marketplace, not individual users.
- When a COTS vendor wrote the marketing literature, it may have had the best of intentions. However, that does not help the user if the advertised feature is not there. Timing is one of the largest issues. A vendor will not know if the solution is successful until the launch is very close, leaving little time and room for correction. Oversights and flawed design work can seriously affect a launch date.
- Except at the end of a build phase during testing, there is no room for feedback anywhere in the process.
- Once development has begun, there is no room for changes.
- If system testing shows that capacity or performance is not adequate it may be impossible to correct.
- With the Waterfall model, requirements are specified, which determine the capabilities. With COTS products, the capabilities determine the requirements, or the delivered system features.

The waterfall model may be fine for smaller projects, but it is not ideal for projects of any size requiring effective executive control. Project managers dealing with IT personnel and executives need a better solution to managing larger projects.

Iterative Process

In other words, this section could be called "deployment of COTS based on iterations." Traditional development involves a waterfall among a series of single, comprehensive phases: design, build, test, and deployment.

Iterative, that is, repetitious, development includes the same phases in the same order. But the phases are not conclusive. Instead, part of the system is designed, built, tested, and (optionally) deployed. Then more of the system is designed, built, tested, and deployed. And the same sequence is followed a third time … and so on.

Iterative development has several advantages over waterfall development, including the ability to learn from issues discovered in later phases to improve the earlier phases in the subsequent iteration, easier adjustment to changes, easier integration, and less pressure on both the contractor and the client to get everything entirely complete before proceeding with the work

Key Factors in the Iterative Process

Key factors in the iterative process include the following:

- Incremental delivery is the key method to an effective iterative process. In traditional waterfall delivery, the entire design is delivered at one time. Then the entire system is built and delivered. Using incremental delivery, the idea is to deliver a well-defined portion of the design and add to that design incrementally in successive iterations of the process. (See the following figure.) You will configure the system in the same way, delivering a working, but unfinished, systems. Then add to and refine that system in subsequent iterations. With each increment, a progressively more complete system will be delivered.

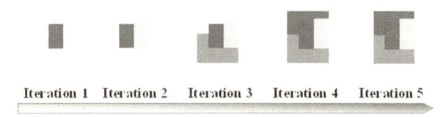

Iteration 1   Iteration 2   Iteration 3   Iteration 4   Iteration 5

Figure 3. Iteration process.

- Rather than attempting to inspect quality via reviews at the end, build it in along the way. It is understood that the line of business and system users must review the work and changes are made as needed. This approach changes the dynamics of these reviews by including key personnel earlier, that is, during the creation process. The reviewers will be responsible for ensuring the system and deliverables reflect line of business and end user concerns and advocating the created system and deliverables in their home organization.

The second and most important part of this process is the "test first" approach. Test scripts are written in advance of any configuration or development, enabling the developers to write just the right amount of code to pass the test case.

- The single home concept for design deliverables means each element has a single home. For example, business processes will live in the business architecture deliverable and only in the business architecture deliverable. If another deliverable discusses a business process, for example, how the configuration of the system relates to how the admin clerk does his or her work, then that deliverable will reference the business process in the business architecture deliverable.

- Everything must be useful in the deliverable document, whether to a group or part of the organization. Intend to ruthlessly eliminate any section that does not clearly have a useful purpose. Doing so will ensure that the development team does not spend time creating sections of low utility. More importantly, customers and end users will not spend any time reviewing such sections.

- Strive for forward movement at all times because it is critical to this process. Rather than waiting for customer approvals before proceeding with the next tasks, move forward. Assume the approvals will be forthcoming. If there are subsequent issues, accept the resulting rework rather than accepting lost waiting time. Where sensible, create a process so you can achieve consensus with business units and customers early rather than attempting approvals late.

- Created and derived from business processes, test cases should begin each iteration as part of exit criteria. Base any special coding or configuration on the test cases and passing that particular test case. This shifts the focus from IT-based thinking to business-based thinking and satisfying the business requirements. This is a change tolerant process. Based on the business model, change can be introduced at any point into the iteration. Impacts can be contained within that iteration or the next.

- Keep the end in mind for all iterations. Most importantly, work on each iteration begins with the definition of objectives in exit criteria for the iteration. This includes the documents for that iteration. The exit criteria will define the scope and purpose of the iteration, the contents for the defined scope, defect tolerances, and completion tolerance. The exit criteria will be presented to the customer for approval at the beginning of each iteration. Move forward. Assume the approvals will be forthcoming.

Iterative Development Overview

The iterative process discussed here is depicted in the following figure. Initially, the component team accepts the responsibility for creating the component deliverable, that is, components. The component team includes both contract and customer personnel.

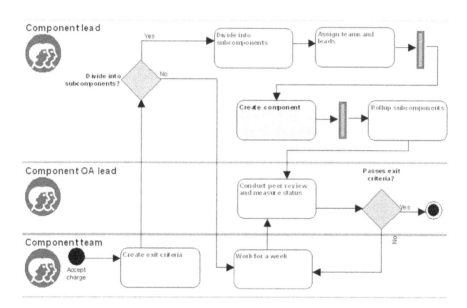

Figure 4. Component deliverable.

The component team creates the exit criteria for the component. The exit criterion for a component is a description of the requirements for the component, that is, what the component must achieve. The exit criterion consists of several sections. It defines the purpose of the component, that is, why this component exists and what it adds to the project. It defines the scope of the component, that is, what is part of this component in this iteration. Often the scope is defined in terms of other components. Exit criteria also define the contents of the component. Typically, this is a high-level outline. Finally, the exit criteria define the defect tolerance of a component. In creating these components, two goals drive us. It is the intent to deliver high-quality documents and systems to the customer. And the team must make progress through the iterations, that is, the team must implement the system in a timely manner.

The method for reconciling these two goals is defining quality thresholds for each component. The quality thresholds determine when a component is finished for each iteration, if needed. Remaining defects are fixed in the development of subsequent iterations.

Once the exit criteria of the component are defined, two things can happen:

- If the component is to be broken into subcomponents, for example, if a volume is to be broken into chapters that are each treated as a separate component, then the component lead will do this division. The component lead is a contract or project person who is responsible for the component through the entire iteration.

- If the component is not to be divided into subcomponents, proceed into a simple loop. The component team works on the component for a week. At the end of the week, the component quality assurance (QA) lead assembles a team to evaluate the status of the component. This person is responsible for the periodic assessment and scoring of this component.

The evaluation of the component is done against the exit criteria. Defects are counted and compared to the quality threshold already defined for the component. If the component deliverable passes, that is, if it has fewer defects than the threshold allows, work associated with that iteration stops on the component. Otherwise, work continues for another week. The component is reviewed again.

Components that are divided into subcomponents each get assigned to their own component team, component lead, and QA lead. Then each subcomponent is worked, as if the process had started from the beginning. Once the subcomponents are finished, the component lead assembles them together. The same kind of weekly assessment is performed on the component as a whole.

While components are in progress, quality assessment scores are provided to all interested parties. In particular, customer and line of business personnel have visibility into the status of a component, the defects it currently has, and its score.

Summary

Each iteration is a small project that connects to other projects. Iterations are change tolerant, that is, a change can be introduced at any point in the process and will be carried over to the next iteration. Testing and QA are essential parts of the iterations. Test cases within the exit criteria of each document ensures the quality as well as just-in-time configuration. The key advantage in the iteration process is that focus remains on moving forward in the project and the ability to change with the business in the course of the project.

Chapter Three

Stakeholders and Change Management

Managing Scope and Stakeholder Expectations

In the iterative process, project scope management can take on an entirely new philosophy and appearance. For traditionally trained managers, this can be a formidable challenge. Even though the intent of the iterative process is to produce the best product possible in the least amount of time and for the least amount of cost, scope management often appears to be more improvisation than controlled execution. In these cases, the traditional decomposition approach to project planning and prediction is not possible.

In traditional software development methodologies, product scope is typically defined in a top-down manner, starting with high-level requirements that are decomposed to more specific requirements. The project manager can use a parallel approach for defining project scope by building a work breakdown structure. This approach gives management a progressively more accurate estimate of the time and cost to complete the project. That is, as the product and work are specified in greater detail, the project estimate becomes more accurate. Once the project's scope baseline has been set, a software manager's main concern for managing scope is guarding constantly against scope creep, especially in the form of product feature changes.

These methods work well when the product definition is not too complex, controversial, or volatile. However, in many cases, the product is excessively difficult to define. In a COTS environment, there is little or no flexibility. These methods are unreliable, misleading, and conflict-ridden. It is no wonder that software developers are willing to adopt a lighter, potentially more effective approach. But where does this leave scope management?

The iterative process values working software over comprehensive documentation and responds to change over following a plan. Alistair Cockburn explained that requirements can be imperfect and design documents and project plans can be outdated. But the project can still succeed by applying such principles as communication and community. This can leave the traditional software project manager adrift in a sea of change, clinging to a frail dinghy lashed together from in-person visits, whiteboard sketches, invention, and light-and-sloppy methods. As scary as this image is, it is not new. In 1989, Gause and Weinberg explored the notion that requirements documents are less important than the process of defining them.

Traditional scope definition has always been a thin security blanket that cannot protect software projects from the crashing waves of scope change in volatile projects. Even under contract, software scope is subject to disputes and threats of litigation. Traditional scope documents, for example, requirements definitions and project plans, do give software management a starting point for negotiating scope changes. Without these, the manager of a COTS deployment project seems to have little to bring to the negotiation table.

Outcome Expectations and Scope Management

The flaw in both traditional and iterative approaches is the assumption that project success is determined by delivering specific product features, whether they are defined hierarchically through decomposition and change management or collaborative iterations. COTS projects are successful only when they have met the stakeholders' expectations. The most important of which are not limited to specific product features. There are three classes of stakeholder expectations: project conduct (project methodology), product (artifact that project produces), and business outcome.

Software development invariably focuses on product expectations as early in the project as possible. Meeting specific product expectations is more predictable, manageable, and, for software builders, more enjoyable than trying to meet either business outcome or project conduct expectations. But this focus on the product exacerbates scope management problems, especially in iterative development. Repeated efforts to get the product functionality just right can lead to extraneous functionality or more elaborate functionality that works against the stakeholders' other expectations. To control scope in iterative development, commit to business outcome expectations as the outer boundaries of scope.

Business outcome expectations are the effects that stakeholders expect the software development project to have on internal operations and/or marketplace or other external environments. An example an operational outcome expectation is reducing inventory errors in manufacturing. An example of an external outcome is capturing a segment of the personal digital assistant (PDA) market. Outcome expectations may align with corporate strategic goals, depending on the clarity, viability, or influence of these goals.

Delivering the right software product features depends ultimately on if those features support the business outcome expectations. This is especially important in iterative projects. Without stable requirements to bolster or burden them, iterative projects need clearly defined and committed business outcome expectations to contain them.

A key control device in configuration is the iteration. Each increment of the product is planned to implement an iteration that represents a set of user functionality. The project sponsor, other users, and development team decide jointly which iteration is to be implemented next and how it will be implemented in product features. The sequence of iterations can wander far from the original intentions for the project. Similarly, the features chosen to implement each iteration are defined iteratively and can also wander. In cases where either the development team or customer is committed to some limited budget or time frame for the overall project, this wandering can lead to problems in funding and deadlines.

This iterative process and many other types of COTS implementation projects are expected to shift direction. Requirements volatility is a primary reason for selecting iterative methodology. But changes can be contained. If the project team has collected, validated, and committed to meet a set of compatible and feasible business outcome expectations, it can use them to open negotiations about which shifts in direction to apply. The project team compares each iteration plan to the committed expectations. Product functionality that is aligned with the overall committed expectations is changed routinely. Changes that contradict or modify the committed expectations are handled as major changes in project scope.

The project team, which includes the project sponsor, commits to selected business outcome expectations early in the project. It repeats this process throughout the project as major changes in the business environment occur. The wording for a business outcome expectation is, "As a result of this project, [some group] will be able to [do something]." A collection of justifications, criteria, and evaluations support this simple statement. Outcome expectations do not refer to a specific product feature, and they do not define specific business functions. This allows the project team leeway in selecting the best detail solutions to meet the expectations.

Not all expectations can be met. Many compete for resources, a few directly contradict each other, and some are not justifiable. The most challenging step in committing to the project's outcome expectations is selecting the expectations to be met. Rejected or deferred expectations introduce risks to the project in terms of distractions and competition. The primary objective of commitment is a consistent vision of the project's success in terms of the expectations that the project is committed to meet. A secondary, but crucial, objective is to develop a plan for mitigating or responding to the risks of deciding not to meet other expectations.

Product Expectations and Outcome Expectations

The relationship between software products and business outcomes is often complex or tenuous, depending on a number of organizational factors. Few sponsors or users can envision the bridge between technology and the overall business outcome, regardless of how well they learn to match technology to immediate functionality. As the manager of an iterative project, you can overtly evaluate these product outcome relationships early in the project. Else, you can rely on users and project sponsors to keep the project on track by guessing.

To control project scope, every product expectation must support a committed business outcome expectation. In any product-centric methodology such as this, check each iteration and product feature against the committed business outcome expectations. When they do not match, the product feature or business function is either out of scope and irrelevant or the committed expectation is out of sync with reality.

Conduct Expectations

Conduct expectations are what the stakeholders expect to experience as part of the project. For iterative projects, the participation of the project sponsor, for example, can be extremely important. But if the project sponsor expects to take a hands-off or infrequent visitor approach to overseeing the project, methodologies such as this cannot be used effectively.

Conduct expectations include the executives' perception of how predictable the completion of the project will be and how much control and/or documentation the project will produce. As with product expectations, project conduct expectations must support the committed business outcome expectations. For example, if your concern for meeting the deadline is tied to a crucial business outcome, then expanding the usual project management activities for an iterative project could be justifiable.

Iterative process challenges software managers and sponsors to relinquish their reliance on comprehensive documentation and intermediate work products. However, without boundaries, the iterative definition and development of product functionality can range out of control. By committing to compatible and feasible business outcome expectations, development teams can manage the scope of iterative projects successfully, resulting in the satisfaction of sponsors, executives, stakeholders, and users.

Stakeholders

Stakeholders, the people who will be impacted by the changes you are introducing, can make or break your projects. Unless businesses truly engage their stakeholders, they are paying one set of employees to initiate change and another to resist it. It is in your interest to manage your stakeholders from the start. Give them a clear, accountable role in change. Then equip them to fulfill it.

Stakeholder management is an important discipline that successful project managers use to win support from others. It helps them ensure that their projects succeed where others fail. Stakeholder analysis is the technique used to identify the key people who have to be won over. You then use stakeholder planning to build the support that helps you succeed. The benefits of using a stakeholder-based approach are that:

- You can use the opinions of the most powerful stakeholders to shape your projects at an early stage. Not only does this make it more likely that they will support you, their input can also improve the quality of your project.

- Gaining support from powerful stakeholders can help you to win more resources. This makes it more likely that your projects will be successful.

- By communicating with stakeholders early and frequently, you can ensure that they fully understand what you are doing and understand the benefits of your project. This means they can support you actively when necessary.

- You can anticipate what people's reaction to your project may be. When you build your plan, you can include the actions that will win people's support.

Stakeholder Analysis

The first step in stakeholder analysis is to identify who your stakeholders are. The next step is to work out their power, influence, and interest so you know who you should focus on. The final step is to develop a good understanding of the most important stakeholders so you know how they are likely to respond and you can work out how to win their support. You can record this analysis on a stakeholder map. The following are the steps to stakeholder analysis:

1. **Identify Your Stakeholders:** The first step in your stakeholder analysis is to identify who your stakeholders are. Think of all the people who are affected by your work, have influence or power over it, or have an interest

in its successful or unsuccessful conclusion. Even though stakeholders may be both organizations and people, you must ultimately communicate with people. Make sure you identify the correct individual stakeholders within a stakeholder organization.

2. **Prioritize Your Stakeholders:** You may now have a long list of people and organizations that are affected by your work. Some of these may have the power to block or advance. Some may be interested in what you are doing. Others may not care. Map out your stakeholders using the following graph. Classify your stakeholders by their power over your work and interest in your work.

High

	Always Listen to	Manage Closely
Power		
	Monitor	Keep Informed

Low

Figure 5. Stakeholder power graph.

Someone's position on the grid shows you the actions you must take with them:

- **High power/Interested people:** Fully engage with these people. Make the greatest efforts to satisfy.

- **High power/Less interested people:** Put in enough work with these people to keep them satisfied. But do not put in so much work that they become bored with your message.

- **Low power/Interested people:** Keep these people adequately informed. Talk to them to ensure that no major issues are arising. Realize that these people can often be very helpful with the detail of your project.

- **Low power/Less interested people:** Monitor these people. But do not bore them with excessive communication.

3. **Understand Your Key Stakeholders:** You now need to know more about your key stakeholders. You need to know how they are likely to feel about and react to your project. You also need to know how best to engage them in your project and how best to communicate with them. The following key questions can help you understand your stakeholders:

- What financial or emotional interest do they have in the outcome of your work? Is it positive or negative?

- What motivates them most of all?

- What information do they want from you?

- How do they want to receive information from you? What is the best way of communicating your message to them?

- What is their current opinion of your work? Is it based on good information?

- Who influences their opinions generally? Who influences their opinion of you? Do some of these influencers therefore become important stakeholders in their own right?

- If they are not likely to be positive, what will win them around to support your project?

- If you do not think you will be able to win them around, how will you manage their opposition?

- Who else might be influenced by their opinions? Do these people become stakeholders in their own right?

A very good way of answering these questions is to talk to your stakeholders directly. People are often quite open about their views. Asking people's opinions is often the first step in building a successful relationship with them.

You can summarize the understanding you have gained on the stakeholder map so you can easily see which stakeholders are expected to be blockers or critics and which stakeholders are likely to be advocates and supporters or your project. Use color coding. For example, show advocates and supporters in green, blockers and critics in red, and neutral people in orange.

Culture Change Management (CCM) Process

In Merriam-Webster, culture is defined as "the ideas, customs, and art of a particular society." For an organization, it could, therefore, be "the ideas, customs, and ways of doing things in the organization." When system or a change in system is introduced, it means, "There will be new ideas, new customs, and new ways of doing things." There may be a culture shock. There will be a change, regardless of your organization's size.

But most people in business give culture change management (CCM), an indifferent response. Skeptics look it as something that is openly emotional or expressive. Some companies say, "Our organization does not need CCM. We've been doing this for years. Anything else new that we introduce around this new system will not be a change. It will be just more of the same … but better!"

Surely, you invest in a new technology because you want to do new things well, not just do the same things better. You want to develop, retain, and grow customer relationships for increased return. Some settle for "more of the same … but better!" Many companies fall into this trap. They replace old technology with newer, faster, smarter technology. Fundamentally, the way that people approach their roles, the processes they use, and the way they do business stays the same.

If you have an expensive Formula One racing car, you would want to experience what it has to offer. You would need to understand it. You would need to be aware of its power and speed. You would need to know how to drive it. You would also need to know how to keep it performing at top speed. You would need to know how to help you win the race and not finish at the same time as the cut-rate car that your competitor bought. If you want to enhance the way your business operates through COTS implementation, then it is vital for your organization to manage the continuous change that will be encountered on this journey.

Change can typically be viewed in number of phases: initiation, uncertainty, and transformation. Each phase will have different actions or variables associated with it. However, when you reach the competence phase, only then will you realize the true benefits of the change introduced.

In the initiation phase, some form of dissatisfaction occurs as a result of internal or external forces, resulting in a change in the organization's vision and values. For change to be initiated, the tension for change must overcome the desire to stay with the status quo. In this example, a decision to change is made.

An uncertainty phase follows. The decision to change then leads to some form of experimenting with what needs to happen. Once an organization has gone through this evaluation and solution development, it introduces the new way via some form of action. This action will often introduce ambiguity or confusion as the organization comes to grips with the new way. Meanwhile, there is a strong desire to not proceed. What's wrong with the way it was? Do we have to change? How hard will it be? Alignment and momentum must be formed to overcome these desires.

When the confusion and ambiguity are removed, the organization starts to see the light at the end of the tunnel in the transformation phase. True transformation starts with creative breakthrough and habitual reframing for the new way. That is, you will mold how things will be done from now on. Desires to go back are diminishing, but some conscious effort is still required to stay on track.

Once the organization has accepted the change, that is, the habits have changed and been accepted, there is no longer a desire to return to the old. Focus grows on how to improve the new ways, leading to mastery and continuous improvement.

In the real world, organizations typically do not identify or understand the issues they face. Most often, they implement change and try to manage it out of sequence.

Many organizations try to introduce continuous improvement while they are still reframing in the breakthrough phase. As a result, some of the organization moves to mastery while some stay stuck in the breakthrough phrase or even revert back to the uncertainty phase … and get stuck there! CCM must happen soon after the project starts. It has to work together with communication, training, and execution plans.

Organizations that want to implement COTS software must be prepared to deal with software modification and workarounds to meet business needs. More importantly, how well will an organization implement the system and deal with changes and the impact this change will have on the organization? When making a selection, organizations tend to focus on a product's technical base. The organization's underlying culture and business processes is equally important. The organization will have to be willing to alter its processes as well as spark, manage, and control change in the organization. Managing culture and process change in large, diverse, organizationally and geographically decentralized companies is a much greater challenge. For more information on this topic, see business process modeling in chapter five.

Leadership must be educated on the importance of change management in a COTS software implementation. Project sponsors must be responsible for assessing organizational readiness, setting expectations, and ensuring accountability. Business processes must change to support new COTS products.

There are two elements that are essential in successful CCM in COTS implementations: project management competence and business involvement.

Project Management Competence

Project management competence is one of the essential tools in COTS implantations. A project manager must possess the following traits of CCM in order to lead a successful implementation:

- Projects tend to be underplanned in CCM areas. Organizational competency to map the complexity of the business process being replaced, understand the politics of change, and manage the change over a sustained period is necessary.

- In large environments, industrial-strength project managers are required to manage the technical program management. In large, complex organizations, project managers must manage communications and change. An added challenge is communicating with multiple oversight bodies.

- The roles of a project manager include managing scope, expectations, complete ownership, culture, and vendor performance. Project managers need to be aware of the project's vital signs. These vary by organization and need to be considered in advance.

- Project managers must use integrated project teams of subject matter experts and contractors. For business units, the project organization has the ultimate responsibility to manage the project.

- Project managers must involve high-level company program managers in defining requirements and making implementation decisions to gain acceptance.

  Project management training and preparation is a must.

Business Involvement

- Business goals must be clearly defined and communicated.

- The organization must be willing and ready to accept the changes to its processes that will result from the new COTS system.

- The health of the organization must be evaluated before, during, and after the implementation as a measure of project risk.

- Change management considerations drive cost and risk. Without dedicated resources for training of senior management, middle management, and users, the project outcome is at risk.

Managing Culture Change Management (CCM) Process

Project and business teams depend on one another for different aspects of the overall change agenda. Project teams identify the changes that are occurring in the business process as a result of implementing the new solution. Business teams validate those changes and make the appropriate organizational and cultural changes to support them. To that end, a project team must complete a gap analysis on process business flows in order to identify changed activities by process flow. In general, the gap analysis identifies four categories of change in activities: new activity, modified activity, existing activity on different system, and existing activity on same system (in case the old system is not being completely replaced).

Additionally, each activity should be annotated with what customization is required to support (if any): new system customization (changes to COTS), existing system modifications, or no system change.

Culture Change Management (CCM) Process Flow

The following diagram illustrates the activities that must occur to successfully identify the change and ensure those changes appropriately feed the training and communications components of the project. The lightly shaded activity boxes at the top of the diagram represent business team activities. The darker-shaded activity boxes at the bottom of the diagram represent project team activities. The activity boxes in the middle with both light and dark shades indicate shared activities. The numbers at each activity box correspond to an activity description in the following table with a step-by-step description of the change process flow diagram.

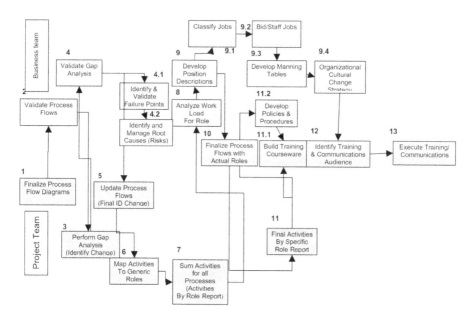

Figure 6. CCM process flow.

Step #	Activity
1	In support of each iteration, the process flows, which are part of business architecture, are finalized.

Step #	Activity
2	Business team validates the process flows as documented. Defects are identified via the quality assessment day (QAD) review process.
3	As process flows are finalized, the project team performs gap analysis and annotates process/activity changes as a result of the implementation of the new system and the integration with existing systems. A complete package identifying the changes is provided to business team.
4	The business team validates the change category identification on the processes listed in 4.1 and 4.2.
4.1	The business team identifies potential failure points and root causes.
4.2	The business team develops risk mitigation strategies for the root causes identified.
5	The business team provides any changes or updates to the project team. The process flow annotations are adjusted.
6	The project team maps all of the validated changes by activity to generic roles that currently exist within the process flows.
7	The project team provides a summary report identifying activities by generic role, such as clerk. These are generated out of the process flow database.
8	The business team analyzes workload by role.
9	The business team develops position descriptions. That is, they define specific roles manifested from the role levels.
9.1	The business team classifies jobs.
9.2	The business team bids or staffs jobs.
9.3	The business team develops manning tables.
9.4	The resulting organizational design drives business team development of the organizational and cultural change strategy.
10	The project and business teams jointly finalize the process flows, updating to incorporate actual final roles as defined by the organizational design.

Step #	Activity
11	The project team produces a final report that identifies all processes or activities by actual job role.
11.1	The project and business teams utilize the processes or activities by actual role to finalize education plans and role-based courseware by iteration.
11.2	The business team utilizes the processes or activities by actual role to feed development of policies and procedures that will be used to support end user training and operation.
12	For future training and communications, the project and business teams identify audiences impacted by these changes.
13	The project and business teams jointly execute on communications and training activities.

Table 3. Change process flow diagram.

Along with all iterations defined for the project, this process will occur iteratively. At the end of the last iteration, a complete and final set of process flows and the corresponding gap analysis will be provided. CCM activities will be accomplished incrementally in alignment with the iterations.

Roles and Responsibilities

- The project team identifies what processes and activities have changed. This activity is based on best industry practices inherent in the COTS software.

- The business team plans and manages the organizational and cultural change to support the process changes, that is, organizational design and development.

- The project team plans. The project and business teams jointly develop training courseware and execute training based on changes in organizational design.

- The project and business team jointly plan and execute communications based on changes in organizational design.

- The project and business teams identify when the change is occurring based on the project plan.

Communication Management

Making the decision to bring a COTS system into your organization is just the first step on a long journey. Although this approach has proven successful for a variety of industries, including manufacturing, transactional, and professional services, the best-laid plans may go awry if the focus is solely on the technical side without considering the cultural and communication aspects of the equation.

Because implementing a new software system usually involves changing human behavior, it is critical to include a carefully constructed communication plan that identifies and addresses human concerns. Initiating transformation of any magnitude across an organization requires meaningful dialogue with executive management, mid-level managers, employees, and other key stakeholders. The leadership team must communicate early and often. These communications must clearly convey the vision, strategies, and benefits for all concerned. Overlooking this piece of the puzzle may undermine your efforts. It could leave employees to fill the gaps with rumor, speculation, and cynicism.

Depending on the existing culture and level of familiarity, the news that a new system is being adopted in the organization may elicit a variety of responses, including everything from fear of the unknown to enthusiastic endorsement.

For some, this new system may represent an unwelcome change in familiar routines. They might say, "We've been doing things the same way for years. Why do we have to switch now?" For others, it may signify opportunity. They might say, "How soon can I sign up for training and start my projects?"

Naturally, there is a wide range of reactions between these two. If you are championing the cause, you will obviously hope to hear comments that lean toward the latter example.

Communication management is one of the essential functions that can dramatically affect the outcome of a project. Project managers must create and effectively use a communication plan that performs two principle functions: collect the right data and disseminate appropriate information in a timely manner. To do this effectively, project teams are under an obligation to identify the appropriate audiences, develop appropriate communication media, establish a communication schedule, and manage the flow of information in and out of the project team.

In this section, we will discuss this process and how this will integrate with the CCM process.

The communications plan outlines a broad framework for effective communications in support of the project. The communications implementation plan is a subplan that extensively defines who, what, where, and how you will effectively communicate to internal and external stakeholders via the defined communications media. The following are some suggestions for the communications plan implementation: monthly project newsletter, communications project messages via the project portal, communications as a result of CCM, or articles, press releases, and project brochures.

Internal Communications

The following table outlines the guidelines and options when creating a project communication plan:

What	Who/Target	Purpose	When/Frequency
Initiation meeting	Stakeholders	• Gather information for initiation plan	• FIRST before project start date
Distribute project initiation plan	Stakeholders	• Distribute plan to alert stakeholders of project scope and gain buy-in	• Before kickoff meeting • Before project start sate
Project kickoff	Stakeholders	• Communicate plans and stakeholder roles/responsibilities • Encourage communication among stakeholders	• At or near project start date
Status reports	Stakeholders	• Update stakeholders on progress of the project	• Regularly scheduled (monthly is recommended for large or mid-size projects)
Team meetings	Entire project team	• Review detailed plans (tasks, assignments, and action items)	• Regularly scheduled (weekly is recommended)

What	Who/Target	Purpose	When/Frequency
Project advisory group meetings	Project advisory group and project manager	• Update project advisory group on status • Discuss critical issues	• Regularly scheduled (monthly is recommended)
Sponsor meetings	Sponsor(s) and project manager	• Update sponsor(s) on status • Discuss critical issues • Seek approval for changes to project plan	• Regularly scheduled (monthly is recommended)
Post-project review	Project Office, Project manager, key stakeholders, and sponsor(s)	• Identify improvement plans and lessons learned (what worked and what could have gone better) • Review accomplishments	• End of project or each major phase
Presentations to special interest groups	Project managers team, leadership groups	• Update external groups to promote communication and create awareness of project interdependencies	• Project milestones
Periodic demonstrations and target presentations	Specific focus groups or end users	• Gain input from special groups and keep them abreast of the project's status	• Once product has enough to present • Completion of critical phases • Complete major enhancements

Table 4. Options for creating a project communication plan.

External Communications

The following is a sample of a communications process. This can be modified to fit the size and scope of many organizations. Keeping stakeholders, employees, and staffers informed will assist with an implementation.

Newsletter

Newsletter (Project X *News*) is published and distributed monthly. The frequency and size of the newsletter, which will consist of five basic sections, should be evaluated on an ongoing basis and adjusted accordingly. The format and content includes the following:

- **Project Status Update:** This section provides status of the project from the project manager's point of view.

- **Spotlight Article**: This section features a focused article on a specific topic of interest, such as iteration functionality. Samples are integration with existing system, training, conversion, and so forth. It may be targeted to specific stakeholder groups.

- **Executive Message**: The executive message will feature a statement of support from a stakeholder at the executive level. The executive will be selected to align with the topic from the spotlight article.

- **Communications Update**: This section informs readers of specific communications-related activities for the current time period, such as presentations, demonstrations, conference participation, executive briefings, and so forth.

- **Kudos**: This section recognizes the outstanding accomplishments of individuals and/or teams. The communications team and editorial board make the nominations.

Production Schedule

The newsletter should be published regularly. Prior to the publishing date, articles must be edited and the newsletter layout must be completed. The edited draft will be distributed to the editorial board, that is, project management and stakeholders, and newsletter communications mail group, that is, the project team, that same day

Roles and Responsibilities

All partners in the project should have responsibility for approving content planning in advance. The goal will be to approve the initial six-month plan as a part of this document. They will revisit with the group each month. An editorial board will represent the partners in approving content planning. The business team will have final approval on each newsletter. The editorial board will be responsible for reviewing the draft edited document and for timely turn around of comments in line with the production calendar.

Authors should come from each part of the project organization. The named author in the newsletter's six-month rolling content schedule should be the lead for the organization that is responsible for that section's content. The author is held accountable for timely submission of the article each month. The named author may designate staff members to contribute to or write articles, as appropriate. The named author identifies a primary backup who is involved in the development of the article each month in the event of an emergency. The backup should be identified to the communications team lead and be included on the six-month rolling calendar.

A newsletter communications mail group will be established. This mail group will include representatives from all of the project's partners. The purpose of this mail group is to allow insight on the articles being written. The newsletter communications mail group is not required to respond, but comments are welcomed.

Web Portal Communications

The project portal should be available to many of the same individuals who are identified for newsletter distribution. Because it also provides open access, standard messages should be provided through this media.

The newsletter will be posted on a link visible from the portal home page. Additionally, the home page should include a project message that will be updated biweekly and managed by the communications team.

The Project Management Office (PMO), communications team, and project teams are all responsible for placing and maintaining content on the portal. Continuous uploading to the portal of project documents is ongoing. The communications team will be responsible for the specific home page message and upload of the newsletter. The PMO will be responsible for uploading any reports. The PMO should be responsible for posting specific project status reports, that is, monthly project status, weekly status report, and other reports deemed useful to communicate the project message.

Summary

Effective communications throughout the project is one of the most effective tools of the project team. Effective communications is summarized as getting the right information to the right people at the right time. We talked about a number of ways this could be accomplished, that is, via newsletters, Web portals, or meetings. Whichever method is chosen, timing and accuracy of the process is essential.

Chapter Four

Architecture

Architectural Mismatches: Approaching Reconciliation

The integration of COTS components into a system under development entails architectural mismatches. This is based on how current business requirements will map to functions provided out of the box in a COTS product. So far, these have been discussed at the component level through component adaptation techniques, but they also must be tackled at an architectural level of abstraction.

In this chapter, we propose an approach for resolving architectural mismatches with the aid of architectural reconciliation. The approach consists of designing and subsequently reconciling two architectural models. One is forward-engineered from the requirements. Another is reverse-engineered from the COTS-based implementation. The final reconciled model is optimally adapted both to the requirements and the actual COTS-based implementation.

This chapter reviews the application of architectural reconciliation in the context of COTS-based software development. Architectural modeling is based on the Unified Modeling Language 2.0 standard, which is widely accepted in the industry. While the reconciliation is performed by transforming the two models, with the help of architectural design decisions.

When reusing COTS components, they simply do not correspond perfectly to the requirements specification and, consequently, the envisioned architecture of the system. Even when COTS-based systems are designed by considering preexisting components from the market that roughly correspond to the requirements, there will still eventually be disparities when the COTS are integrated. One of the major causes of this problem is architectural mismatches. There are differences between a COTS component and the software system and where it will be integrated, which occur when the former makes the wrong assumptions about the latter.

For example, a commercial component can falsely assume that it is in charge of controlling the sequence of interactions between itself and other components or other components should comply with specific protocols of interactions. A good example of this process is in financial systems that post transactions to general ledger systems. Not understanding which component is in charge could result in missing or duplicate information in total numbers. To make matters worse, such assumptions are implicit and usually conflict with each other. Consequently, system-wide properties are diverged from the requirements, both functional and quality ones. Quality requirements, such as performance, reliability, and flexibility, which depend profoundly on the architecture, may be, to a large extent, distressed by the use of COTS components.

Many software implementation groups have attempted to tackle the problem of architectural mismatches. They focus on the component level via component adaptation techniques, which try to incorporate unintended changes in a component for use in a particular application. These techniques are distinguished into white box and black box, depending on if the component itself is adapted or if its interface is adapted. In the case of COTS components, black-box techniques are usually applied since the component's source code is usually prohibited from being inspected or modified.

But architectural mismatches cannot only be resolved at the component level because they do not concern an isolated component. Instead, they affect a greater part of the system, which collectively includes a number of components and connectors. Architectural mismatches caused by a single component may influence the components that communicate with it as well as spread further on to other components. Such mismatches may require the adaptation of the COTS component as well as the modification, addition, or removal of other architectural elements. In order to perform these changes, we need to examine a greater part of the system's architecture, identify those elements that are affected, and subsequently decide on how exactly the architecture should be modified. Essentially, we need to tackle the problem of architectural mismatches from an architectural perspective.

This process proposes an approach to resolve architectural mismatches that are caused by integrating COTS. We will use the technique of architectural reconciliation from the University of Luxembourg. Specifically, their paper suggests the design and, subsequently, the reconciliation of two architectural models. One is forward engineered from the requirements specification. The second is reverse-engineered from the COTS-based system implementation. The former expresses the architectural decisions in an ideal system, which conforms to the requirements. Not only does the latter grasp the implementation constraints, it also explicitly specifies the architectural impact of COTS that were incorporated in the implementation, making their design assumptions explicit with respect to the rest of the application.

These two models are reconciled into a third model that will combine the two perspectives in the best possible trade-off by considering the design assumptions of the COTS components. But it will also address the requirements to the best possible extent. The reconciliation is performed by transforming the two models, based on architectural design decisions, depending on which side, requirements, or implementation should be more supported. The reconciled model can eventually be used to reengineer the COTS-based system and update the requirements. Architectural modeling is based upon the UML 2.0 standard. This is one of the best approaches I have seen in the current academia environments.

The process of reconciliation is graphically illustrated in the following figure. It is comprised of six consecutive phases.

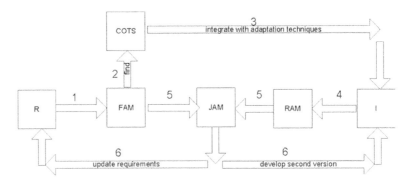

Figure 7. Process of Architectural Reconciliation.

The first three phases follow a simplistic, forward-engineering style.

1. The process commences by using the requirements specification (R) to design the ideal architecture of the system, or the Forward Architectural Model (FAM). This model should, if possible, consider preexisting COTS from the market that essentially correspond to the requirements.

2. In sequence, commercial components are located in the market, that is, if they haven't already been found.

3. Eventually the implementation (I) is developed according to the FAM, by building new components from scratch and by including the COTS found. At the best-case scenario, the COTS components will be adapted at a component level according to one of the aforementioned component adaptation techniques.

4. The fourth phase is to reverse-architect the COTS-based implementation in order to recover its architecture, or the Reverse Architectural Model (RAM).

Obviously, reverse-architecting is a special case of reverse-engineering, which concerns only architectural design. Here, similarly as before, we do not prescribe a specific reverse-architecting approach, but a few such techniques and tools are proposed, such as those in that will be discussed later.

5. The most crucial phase is to bridge the RAM and FAM into the Joint Architectural Model (JAM), which must compromise between the COTS-based implementation and set of ideal requirements. This is achieved by performing a transformation, which accepts the RAM and the FAM as inputs and produces the JAM as the output. A necessary trade-off must be made because it is highly impossible to perfectly satisfy the requirements, especially the nonfunctional or quality requirements. The transformation enforces a set of design decisions that resolve the incompatibilities between the RAM and FAM. Specifically, the architect must go through the following steps:

   a. Identify the architectural mismatches between the RAM and FAM. To start, the architect must look for the four different kinds of false assumptions that integration of COTS components may entail. These assumptions may lead to architectural mismatches or, more simply, differences between the FAM and RAM, that must be explicitly specified. The architectural mismatches can be detected by comparing the RAM and FAM either informally, for example, via UML diagrams, or more formally, for example, via formal models with precise semantics.

   b. Resolve the architectural mismatches. By resolving the architectural mismatches, the architect needs to decide between one of the following options. Keep the part of the FAM and delete the part of the RAM that causes the mismatch, if enforcing the requirements is more significant. Or, keep the part of the RAM and delete the part of the FAM that causes the mismatch, if requirements can be compromised in favor of the COTS components. Generate a trade-off solution that mixes both parts. In this case, some of the elements from both models may be deleted. Others may be retained and possibly modified while more elements may be added. Component adaptation techniques can be again enforced here, if it is necessary to adapt the behavior of COTS components.

   c. Complete the JAM. The resolution of the architectural mismatches will probably have consequences to other architectural elements that were not themselves part of the problem. Therefore, the software architect needs to make some last-minute decisions with respect to keeping, deleting, or modifying architectural elements that the reconciliation actions affected.

6. The final phase in this process is to reengineer the system according to the JAM and update the requirements document to reflect the changes that occurred during the reconciliation. Our goal in this process was not to invent yet another forward-engineering or reverse-architecting process. Instead, we wanted to focus on the reconciliation of architectural models.

The Architectural Description

An architectural description is comprised of multiple views: the component-connector view, logical view, implementation view, data view, and deployment view. In order to reduce the complexity of bridging two complex, multiple-view architectural models, we have focused on the component-connector view for two reasons. First, it is considered to contain the most significant architectural information. Second, it is the most appropriate view to describe COTS components. This view deals with the system run-time by showing the components, units of run-time computation or data storage, and connectors, the interaction mechanisms between components.

For the language describing the architecture, UML has been selected to accomplish this task. The emergent and integration of UML 2.0 standards describe the component-connector view and especially chose modeling elements from the composite structures and components packages, namely components, connectors, interfaces, ports, and classes that belong to the internal structures of components. In UML 2.0, components are associated with provided and required interfaces. They may own ports that formalize their interactions points. A special case of connectors, that is, assembly connectors, connect the required interface of one component to the provided interface of a second.

Architecture Teams and Responsibilities

You should include an architecture team as part of the project structure. This team is broken down into two distinctive groups: the business architecture team and technical architecture team.

Business Architecture Team

The business architecture team performs business analysis, completes the business system and business process modeling, and develops the business architecture document (BAD) component deliverable along with associated artifacts. The team models internal business workers and the information they use (business entities), key business goals, events, strategies, and business workers' structural organization into independent units (business systems). The team defines how they interact in workflow-related business activities to realize the behavior described in business processes.

The business architecture-related artifact set, for which the business architecture team is responsible, includes the following: vision (RUP), business process specification (document), business information model, glossary (RUP), business process flows, location model, organization models, business event models, and business strategy model.

The business architecture team is also responsible for the business architecture document (BAD), a component deliverable.

Traceabilities

As part of the standard UML model process, the business activities, which comprise the business architecture and related processes, are captured in the business model. They are traceable to the COTS system by using use cases within the project's UML use case model (UCM) and presented within the software requirements specification (SRS) component. This trace mapping between business activities and system use cases is maintained via business modeling attribution.

Technical Architecture Team

The technical architecture team's responsibilities are twofold:

1. Perform system software-related requirements analysis, modeling, and documentation activities, including:

   - System use case modeling

   - Use case specification and activity modeling

   - Tracing the UCM's use cases to their respective business process activity counterparts

   - Developing, refining, and maintaining the SRS component deliverable

2. Perform system architectural analysis, design modeling, and documentation activities, including:

   - Completing architectural analysis and modeling toward realizing the architecturally significant use cases, which the team's architects selected from the UCM, within the analysis model (AM)

   - Realizing the architecturally significant use cases in the AM via development of views of participating classes (VOPC) analysis class diagrams and interaction diagrams (sequence or collaborations)

- Developing analysis views with explicit trace dependencies between the use cases, their AM realizations, which are comprised of AM VOPC class diagrams and associated interaction diagrams
- Through subsequent stages of refinement, generating design model (DM) realizations along with explicit DM views tracing both the UCM and AM realizations to their DM counterparts
- Developing, refining, and maintaining the software architecture document (SAD), a component deliverable using the architecturally significant UCM along with the AM and DM realizations of these use cases

The requirements management-related artifact set, for which the technical architecture team is responsible, includes the following:

- Software requirements specification (RUP)
- Use case model sample tool (Rational Rose Enterprise suite by IBM)
- Business process activity to use case mapping (modeling tool set)
- Supplementary specifications (RUP)
- Use case specification (RUP)

The analysis, design model-related artifact set, for which the technical architecture team is responsible, includes the following:

- Data conversion plan
- SAD (RUP)
- AM (Rational Rose Enterprise suite by IBM)
- DM (Rational Rose Enterprise suite by IBM)
- Implementation model (Rational Rose Enterprise suite by IBM)
- Deployment model (Rational Rose Enterprise suite by IBM)
- Logical information model (Rational Rose Enterprise suite by IBM; data modeling tool)
- Technical standards

Component deliverables include the following:

- SRS
- UCM views
- Use case specifications
- Supplemental requirements
- Business process activity to use case mapping

- SAD
- Architecturally significant UCM views
- AM views, including those associated with use case AM realization, that is, participating AM classes' structure views and their interaction views
- Use case to AM realization mappings
- DM views, including those associated with use case DM realization, that is, participating DM classes' structure views and their interaction views
- Use case AM realization to DM realization mappings
- Implementation model views

Traceability Mapping

The project use cases within the project's UCM and presented within the SRS component are traced forward to their related business process activities presented in the BAD. These use cases are also traced to both the AM and DM realizations. These trace mappings are established and maintained within the project's UML model using the Rational Rose Enterprise suite by IBM. This mapping is done using explicitly stereotyped trace dependencies within the model's configured units. All of which are maintained under configuration management and configuration.

- SRS Component Traceability
  - Use case(s) to business process activity
  - Logical screen, screen definition to use case
- SAD Component Traceability
  - Use case to AM realizations, which include:
    - Views of participating AM classes (VOPC)
    - Views of sequence interactions and/or collaborations among these participating AM classes
  - AM realization to DM realization views with explicit trace dependencies
    - AM view boundary classes trace to DM screen or reports or form design classes, which, in turn, trace to the DM web server subsystem
    - AM controller boundary classes traced to the DM application server subsystem, component, and (deployment) node views

- AM external interface boundary classes trace to the DM interface port classes, which, in turn, trace to the DM application server supporting the system interfaces to external systems
- AM domain entity classes traced to the DM CBO/cache server subsystem

Architecture Framework

During the course of the project, work products that are created and iteratively extended to address a significant subset of the thirty potential cells in the commonly used Zachman framework. In 1987, John Zachman, author of the Zachman Framework for Enterprise Architecture, wrote "To keep the business from disintegrating, the concept of information systems architecture is becoming less of an option and more of a necessity." From that assertion over 15 years ago, the Zachman Framework for Enterprise Architecture has evolved and become the model around which major organizations view and communicate their enterprise information infrastructure. The Zachman Framework draws upon the discipline of classical architecture to establish a common vocabulary and set of perspectives, a framework, for defining and describing today's complex enterprise systems. Enterprise Architecture provides the blueprint, or architecture, for the organization's information infrastructure. You should expect these work products to support the information architecture and enterprise architecture requirements. The remaining six cells, which are shaded in blue, are determined to address a level of detail that is not appropriate for a COTS implementation.

	DATA What	FUNCTION How	NETWORK Where	PEOPLE Who	TIME When	MOTIVATION Why
SCOPE (CONTEXTUAL) Planner	List of Business Entities BAD	List of Business Processes BAD	List of Locations BAD	List of Organizations BAD	List of Business Events BAD	List of Business Goals BAD
ENTERPRISE MODEL (CONCEPTUAL) Owner	Business Data Structure Model & Glossary BAD	Business Process Flows BAD	Location Model BAD	Organizational Model BAD	Business Event Model BAD	Business Strategy Model BAD
SYSTEM MODEL (LOGICAL) Designer	System Logical Info Model & Glossary SAD	Use Case Model, SRS Analysis Model SAD	Technical Standards, Deployment Model SAD	Use Case Model, SRS Analysis Model SAD	Activity Diagram per System Use Case SRS	Business Rules, Supplementary Requirements Spec BAD
TECHNOLOGY MODEL (PHYSICAL) BUILDER	Interface Definitions, (COTS) Config Spec	Design Model (COTS) SAD	Deployment Model SAD	Human Interface Boundary Classes SAD	Sequence Diagrams (COTS) SAD	
DETAILED REPRESENTATIONS (OUT-OF-CONTEXT)				Security Specification Security Plan		

Table 5. Zachman Framework.

Summary

COTS-based software development entails architectural mismatches that must be dealt with at a component level through component adaptation techniques as well as at the architectural level. By doing so, we can examine a number of components and their connectors in a group, making modifications to a considerable part of the system's architecture. We have thus proposed to design two architectural models. The first is based on the requirements. The second is based on the existing implementation. Then we reconcile these two models through a trade-off decision process. The added value of this approach concerns the adoption of architectural reconciliation in the context of COTS-based software development in order to resolve architectural mismatches at an architectural level.

We have also discussed the project structure and the architectural teams and their roles in the process and how they satisfy the Zachman requirements. It is noteworthy that architectural teams are an intricate part of the project from start to finish.

Chapter Five

Business-driven Implementation

Introduction

Companies today need to keep up with the pace at which the competitive market demands new business capabilities. Based on research by various business groups and personal experience, approximately 80 percent of a company's IT budget is spent either maintaining or enhancing existing applications. These existing applications were not created with flexibility in mind. Hence, while the business is leapfrogging with new and enhanced processes, the IT backbone is incapable of honoring the required changes. Traditional applications and architectures are unable to keep up with business innovation. This is primarily because the processes are not adaptable to business needs on demand.

Business requirements often get transformed into separate IT projects that cannot work together. Reusability between artifacts created for different IT projects is often very low. Creating applications that are flexible enough to react to the unknown requires a more systematic approach toward application development. With the business unable to create IT functionality that is capable of reacting to the unknown, it has traditionally been very difficult to justify the deeper budgetary requirement to create flexible IT applications. The traditional inflexibility of application architectures makes even small improvements so expensive that they become virtually impossible to justify.

IT teams can devise a method by which IT efforts are interlocked with business strategy and requirements through an execution framework that is standardized and well-understood and can be executed repeatedly and successfully. The enterprise might achieve business flexibility through IT by modeling the business processes that collectively define the way the business executes.

First, model a business process through its constituent process steps. By measuring a business process or a key use case through return on investments (ROIs),

44

key performance indicators (KPIs), or other metrics, the enterprise can use these business process models (BPMs) as an essential mechanism to communicate the business needs to the IT realm. The business and IT can significantly bridge the communication chasm by using well-articulated BPMs that create a link between what the business needs and what IT implements and delivers.

While the starting step for business-driven implementation (BDI) is the creation of BPMs, the IT solution structure also needs to adapt to using the BPMs as input artifacts to the design and development phases of the SDLC. The IT architecture needs to be able to design and implement the process activities as software components or services.

By using BDI, the enterprise models and provides new business processes, when conceptualized, to the IT department. Analysis of the new process might reveal that software services might already exist to address the need and the only work effort required is to wire the existing software services to realize the new business process. Or, it might reveal that the enterprise needs to implement new software services and add them to the IT service portfolio. Similarly, if changes are needed to an existing process, the BPM is revamped to reflect the change. It is then delivered to IT for subsequent technical revision, based on which services might need to be enhanced or modified.

A BDI approach helps increase the agility of the business and prioritize and align IT initiatives with business imperatives. It also indirectly helps in simplifying the process of cost justification for IT budgets within an enterprise.

The Execution Model

Enterprise IT groups should strive to bridge the gap between business needs and IT solutions as well as be agile and responsive in creating IT solutions. This need has led to the development of a services-oriented architecture (SOA), which provides an IT framework along with a set of principles and guidelines to create IT solutions as a set of reusable, composable, and configurable services that are independent of applications and run-time platforms. Transitioning an enterprise to SOA requires a BDI approach that uses business goals and requirements to drive downstream design, development, and testing. This promises to create composite business applications by reusing existing or newly created services, which helps to create adaptable and flexible business solutions. It also brings a much needed flexibility in enterprise IT and helps to align IT solutions with business needs.

First, model the business processes that need IT enablement. Preferably, to start, model the key business processes. Communicate the business requirements to the IT domain by using the outputs of the modeling activity. It is the responsibility of the business users and stakeholders to associate the processes and its significant steps with ROI, KPI, and any other pertinent metric. In the later stages of the IT life cycle, this will help to validate that IT delivered what the business proposed.

Once the processes are modeled, the outputs of the models can be used as inputs to an initiative's requirements gathering phase. The activities or process steps that comprise a given business process model can be analyzed to form the basis of use case modeling. Developing use cases is a significant step in a project's requirement gathering phase. Based on the use cases, the application architecture is structured. The enterprise services are identified, designed, developed, and subsequently wired together as service composites that realize the business processes. After development, the project moves to the deployment stage. During which, the developed components are exposed as publishable, location-transparent, and discoverable services. These software services are deployed to an execution run time, for example, an application server.

In post-deployment, the project enters the monitoring or management phase. Once they are up and running, business processes can be monitored for real-time performance and data capture, reporting, and analysis. For this to happen, the steps in the business process, as modeled in the first step, need to be assigned various business metrics, for example, ROI and KPI. Against these metrics, run-time performance, latency, and other factors can be measured. Measurement is essential to validate if the IT solution meets the needs of the business as defined by a service level agreement (SLA).

Data obtained from the run-time monitoring is analyzed against the expected SLA or other benchmark performance metrics and criteria. The captured information is provided to the architects, designers, and developers, who then analyze the data and find innovative ways of optimizing or improving the process through enhancements and performance tuning of implementation code. Sometimes, the business users might make the changes. They will change business rules using external interfaces, which does not require any code changes.

If the analysis suggests changes to be made in the business process, the corresponding process models can be modified. The same steps, that is, develop, deploy, and then monitor, can be repeated to enhance the implementation. This completes the execution loop with analysis and process adaptation techniques feeding back to the modeling step. This mechanism helps both the business and IT adapt to the changing business needs with quick turnaround time. It helps justify cost enhancements to existing system functionality by directly associating business needs and justification to a given IT initiative.

Modeling Business Processes

Modeling business processes are comprised of dozens of discrete business components. Process workflows, business use case specifications, deployment models, and reusable code are all types of business process flows. When they are organized in a clear format and related within a RUP or UML format, you can see clearly the cause-effect relationships and how work really gets done throughout the business unites affected by your project. Nothing is hidden behind organizational walls or disappears into a black box. You can codify how things get done in support of key goals while exploiting best practices and industry standards. The following components should be included in the business modeling process:

Strategy Layer	Business case Value proposition Capabilities roadmap
Business Process	Business interaction model As-is process flows To-be process flows Business scenarios
Application Architecture	Software architecture document Use cases Information flow diagrams Data model Data dictionary User interface prototypes Application demo models
Infrastructure	Program overview Strategy Conceptual design Reference architecture Costing model

Table 6. Components included in the business modeling process.

Multidimensional Business Model (MDBM)

Historically, business models have been a hierarchical representation of the organizational structure, which related little to timeliness, cost, and quality issues.

True business improvement is driven by optimizing the processes that a business performs. A business process represents how work gets done in the organization. Rather than looking at the organization vertically, that is, using a hierarchy, the correct view of the business is taken horizontally. In other words, the business processes that flow across organizational boundaries are analyzed.

By nature, a business process is initiated by an event that consumes resources, performs activities, and produces goods or services. The event component of the business process allows for the analysis of timeliness issues. The resources consumed allows for the analysis of associated costs. The activities performed leads to analysis targeting process quality. Finally, the resulting goods and services lead to the analysis of product quality.

In an iterative process, one of the most important aspects of the process is documenting and presenting the current and future state business processes horizontally. This is best represented by creation of a BPM for both states of the business. An active BPM model can be used in two distinctive ways.

1. The BPM will help business owners understand current and future state. This will also enable them to do "what if" analysis on business scenarios.

2. When applied correctly in a UML process, the BPM will enable you to create use cases.

When modeling a business process, you should take a business-centric approach, not a technical one. Experts advocate breaking down a process into the major grouping of its parts so it can be understood better. That approach forms the basis of a multidimensional business model (MDBM). To create a cohesive MDBM, your approach should consist of asking the five "w" series of questions: why, what, who, where, and when.

- **Why:** This is the reason a business unit or process exists. For example, a process could exist to improve business communications with a corporation's trading partner. Having the latest and greatest technology available is not sufficient reason for creating a project. You have to start with the business requirement.

- **What:** This considers the detailed business activities that must be accomplished to achieve the goal of the process.

- **Who:** This step requires two steps. First, the "what" activities are dissected. A hierarchy of actions that comprise those activities is created. Then, MDBM looks at who is responsible for each of those actions.

- **Where:** This step looks at where actions or activities are performed using that business model.

- **When:** This step requires you to look at the timeline of the business process and identify all the time frames that actors must be compliant within the process. You can then create a model that says what information you need to accomplish this activity at this place and point in time.

Once these questions are answered, your modelers will have a very rigorous set of specifications. They can take the output from MDBM and translate it into the UML. MDBM provides a set of data about the business process; UML draws on a couple of the dimensions of MDBM. The result is a model of the business in its current state. Projects can use this model to map future state processes based on the application and requirements.

UML alone cannot provide the versatility that MDBM can offer. UML models are very good for technical users, but business users usually miss the underlying point of them. MDBM is simple, but it is a powerful presentation of the business process in a way that nontechnical business users can understand and relate to.

The next step is process step modeling, where you work out how processes outlined in the top-level view are performed, that is, the sequence of steps, what actions are performed, what information is created, what relationships are created between information, where the decision points are in the process, and exceptions. Modeling exceptions is crucial. The flow of the MDBM within each swim lane, a technique for mapping organizational structure to processes, is not much of an issue. However, the exceptions usually cause confusion within the model.

Another dimension in the system enables modelers to create views that can be created into the process model to show where an application appears in the process and how it works. This links the process model inherently into the application definition. The next part allows modelers to link to a specific component within the application to provide a detailed view of the workflow between the human part of the process and the specific components of the model being built.

Capturing the Business Process

Business analysts, rather than IT staff, should model business processes. Each iteration team should include business analysts and architects from the start just for this reason. A complete MDBM model should contain the following dimensions:

- Workflow dimension models define a process's initiating events, its flow of work, the actors responsible for performance, and the resulting deliverables produced by its activities. As-is and to-be models may be built for purposes of redesigning and improving the process. Once defined in a workflow model, a process may be simulated to analyze its performance in terms of cost, timing, and resource constraints. A workflow model gives a more detailed view of a business process, helping you visualize and analyze how multiple departments or organizational units work together by evaluating their internal activities and the passing of deliverables among them. A workflow model represents a business process in terms of its component activities and flow of work among the activities. A workflow model concentrates on the flow of work through the business for a single output, that is, a product or service, or a single input, that is, the handling of an order. Because processes often cross organizational boundaries, the workflow model depicts the organizational components performing each activity and the workflow, that is, deliverables and/or events, between the activities.

- An event dimension model is a hierarchy that organizes the events that are of importance to the business. The event modeler provides a facility for categorizing the events that the business uses in a hierarchy. A general event is placed at the highest level of the model. This is the model's root. More specific events are organized below it to support or further describe the root. The lower in the hierarchy the event appears, the more detailed the event. Events trigger the commencement of processes or activities from which a planned response or deliverable is produced.

- A process dimension model defines the project's functional processes and activities. Included in this set of modelers is a process modeler to show functional hierarchy and a use case modeler to show process components and their organizational usage requirements. Once inventoried and defined, these process components can be used to construct process workflow models. A process' workflow model shows when and how its activities are performed, what inputs it consumes, and what outputs it delivers.

- A use case dimension model represents how systems and organizational components, that is, markets, organizations, roles, and people, interact with a process or activity to receive deliverables that are of value to them. A use case model simplifies analysis by logically partitioning the business into portions that service these interactions. For each interaction, the use case model can specify the external actors who are involved, the nature of the interaction that takes place, and the portion of the business supporting the interaction.

- The sequence dimension model details how a use case, that is, activity or business process, is realized by communicating objects. When the process is initiated, the sequence model illustrates the business classes whose instances are involved, the time-sequenced messages between these classes, and the operations performed on each class instance in response to a message.

- An operation dimension model profiles an operation's algorithm. At its highest level, this profile simply identifies other operations that the subject operation communicates with, that is, sends messages to. Operation models are typically developed to detail the business domain's behavior in response to an event. The focus of an operation model is an operation that is invoked as the result of some event realized by the business domain. During the performance of the topic operation, it may request other operations to assist in accomplishing its function. These requests take the form of messages, which solicit operations from their own business classes or other classes. In turn, these requested operations may request other operations. The optional further levels of detail become increasingly algorithmic as sequence, repetition, and condition are added. This unfolds the dynamics of operation interaction. Operations models may be coupled together to show a more complete picture of the cascading effect of messaging. A good example of this process is in a simple shopping Web site. The business process of taking the order is modeled. This model, coupled with technical details of the same process, would create a more complete view of the entire process.

Requirement Types

Software system requirements are often classified in the following groups: functional requirements, nonfunctional requirements, domain requirements, user requirements, and system requirements.

Functional Requirements

Functional requirements are statements of services the system should provide. They also detail how the system should react to particular inputs and how the system should behave in particular situations. In some cases, the functional requirements may also explicitly state what the system should not do. The functional requirements for a system describe what the system should do. These requirements depend on the type of software being developed, the expected users of the software, and the general approach that the organization takes when writing requirements.

When expressed as user requirements, the requirements are usually described in a fairly abstract way. However, functional system requirements describe the system function in detail, its inputs and outputs, exceptions, and so on. Functional requirements for a software system may be expressed several ways. These functional user requirements define specific facilities that the system will provide. In principle, the functional requirements' specification of a system should be both complete and consistent. Complete means that all services that the user requires should be defined. Consistent means that requirements should not have contradictory definitions.

In practice, for large, complex systems, it is practically impossible to achieve requirements that are consistent and complete. It is easy to make mistakes and omit things when writing specifications for these types of systems. In addition, different system stakeholders have different and often inconsistent needs.

These inconsistencies may not be obvious when the requirements are first specified, so inconsistent requirements are included in the specification. The problems may only emerge after deeper analysis. Sometimes, they emerge after development is complete and the system is delivered to the customer.

Nonfunctional Requirements

Nonfunctional requirements are not directly concerned with the specific functions that the system delivers. They may relate to emergent system properties, including reliability, response time, and store occupancy. Alternatively, they may define constraints on the system such as the capabilities of I/O devices and the data representations used in system interfaces. Nonfunctional requirements are rarely associated with individual system features. Rather, these requirements specify or constrain the emergent properties of the system. Therefore, they may specify system performance, security, availability, and other emergent properties.

They are often more critical than individual functional requirements. System users can usually find ways to work around a system function that does not really meet their needs. However, failing to meet a nonfunctional requirement can mean the whole system is unusable. For example, if an aircraft system does not meet its reliability requirements, it will not be certified as safe for operation. If a real-time control system fails to meet its performance requirements, the control functions will not operate correctly.

Nonfunctional requirements are not just concerned with the software system to be developed. Some nonfunctional requirements may constrain the process that should be used to develop the system.

Examples of process requirements include: a specification of the quality standards that should be used in the process, a specification that the design must be produced with a particular toolset, and a description of the process that should be followed.

Nonfunctional requirements arise through user needs because of budget constraints, organizational policies, the need for interoperability with other software or hardware systems, or external factors such as safety regulations or privacy legislation.

The types of nonfunctional requirements are product requirements, organizational requirements, and external requirements.

Product requirements specify product behavior. Examples include:

- Performance requirements on how fast the system must execute and how much memory it requires
- Reliability requirements that set out the acceptable failure rate
- Portability requirements
- Usability requirements

Organizational requirements are derived from policies and procedures in the customer's and developer's organization. Examples include:

- Process standards that must be used
- Implementation requirements, for example, the programming language or design method used
- Delivery requirements that specify when the product and its documentation are to be delivered

The broad heading of external requirements covers all requirements that are derived from factors external to the system and its development process. These may include:

- Interoperability requirements that define how the system interacts with systems in other organizations
- Legislative requirements that must be followed to ensure the system operates within the law
- Ethical requirements

Ethical requirements are placed on a system to ensure it will be acceptable to its users and the general public. These are constraints on the services or functions that the system offers. They include timing constraints, constraints on the development process, and standards.

Nonfunctional requirements often apply to the system as a whole. They do not usually just apply to individual system features or services. However, nonfunctional requirements can be difficult to verify. Users often state these requirements as general goals, for example, ease of use, the ability of the system to recover from failure, or rapid user response. These vague goals cause problems for system developers as they leave scope for interpretation and subsequent dispute once the system is delivered.

Whenever possible, you should write nonfunctional requirements quantitatively so they can be objectively tested. You can measure these characteristics when the system is being tested to check if the system has met its nonfunctional requirements.

In practice, however, customers for a system may find it impossible to translate their goals into quantitative requirements. For some goals, such as maintainability, there are no metrics that can be used. In other cases, even when quantitative specification is possible, customers may not be able to relate their needs to these specifications. They do not understand what some number defining the required reliability means in terms of their everyday experience with computer systems. Furthermore, the cost of objectively verifying quantitative nonfunctional requirements may be very high. The customers paying for the system may not think these costs are justified. Therefore, requirements documents often include statements of goals mixed with requirements. These goals may be useful to developers because they indicate the customers' priorities. But you should always tell customers that they are open to misinterpretation and cannot be objectively verified.

Nonfunctional requirements often conflict and interact with other functional or nonfunctional requirements. For example, it may be a requirement that the maximum memory used by a system should be no more than four megabytes. Memory constraints are common for embedded systems where space or weight is limited and the number of memory chips storing the system software must be minimized.

It is helpful if you can differentiate functional and nonfunctional requirements in the requirements document. In practice, this is difficult to do. If the non-functional requirements are stated separately from the functional requirements, it is sometimes difficult to see the relationships between them. If they are stated with the functional requirements, you may find it difficult to separate functional and nonfunctional considerations as well as identify requirements that relate to the system as a whole. But you should explicitly highlight requirements that are clearly related to emergent system properties, such as performance or reliability. Put them in a separate section of the requirements document. Or, distinguish them in some way from other system requirements.

Domain Requirements

Domain requirements come from the application domain of the system. They reflect characteristics and constraints of that domain. In reality, they may be functional or nonfunctional requirements, but the distinction between different types of requirements is not as clear-cut as these simple definitions suggest. A user requirement concerned with security may appear to be a nonfunctional requirement. However, when developed in more detail, this requirement may generate other requirements that are clearly functional, such as the need to include user authentication facilities in the system.

Domain requirements are derived from the application domain of the system rather than from the specific needs of system users. They usually include specialized domain terminology or refer to domain concepts. They may be new functional requirements in their own right, constrain existing functional requirements, or set out how particular computations must be carried out. Because these requirements are specialized, software engineers often find it difficult to understand how they are related to other system requirements.

Domain requirements are important because they often reflect fundamentals of the application domain. If these requirements are not satisfied, it may be impossible to make the system work satisfactorily.

User Requirements

The user requirements for a system should describe the functional and nonfunctional requirements so system users understand them without detailed technical knowledge. They should only specify the external behavior of the system. They should avoid, as far as possible, system design characteristics.

Consequently, if you are writing user requirements, you should not use software jargon or structured or formal notations. You should not describe the requirement by describing the system implementation. Write user requirements in simple language with simple tables and forms and intuitive diagrams. For example, a good requirement would be: "In order for the customer to validate his or her address, the system must present an address conformation screen."

However, various problems can arise when requirements are written in natural language sentences in a text document. For example:

- **Lack of clarity:** It is sometimes difficult to use language in a precise, unambiguous way without making the document wordy and difficult to read.

- **Requirements confusion:** Functional requirements, nonfunctional requirements, system goals, and design information may not be clearly distinguished.

- **Requirements computation:** Several different requirements may be expressed together as a single requirement.

System Requirements

System requirements are expanded versions of the user requirements that software engineers use as the starting point for the system design. They add detail and explain how the system should provide the user requirements. They may be used as part of the contract for the implementation of the system. Therefore, they should be a complete and consistent specification of the whole system.

Ideally, the system requirements should simply describe the external behavior of the system and its operational constraints. They should not be concerned with how the system should be designed or implemented. However, at the level of detail required to completely specify a complex software system, it is impossible, in practice, to exclude all design information. There are several reasons for this:

- You may have to design an initial architecture of the system to help structure the requirements specification. The system requirements are organized according to the different subsystems that make up the system.

- In most cases, systems must interoperate with other existing systems. These constrain the design. These constraints impose requirements on the new system.

- The use of a specific architecture to satisfy nonfunctional requirements may be necessary. An external regulator who needs to certify that the system is safe may specify that an architectural design that has already been certified be used. Natural language is often used to write system requirements specifications as well as user requirements.

Because system requirements are more detailed than user requirements, natural language specifications can be confusing and hard to understand. Understanding natural language relies on the specification that readers and writers use the same words for the same concept. This leads to misunderstandings because of the ambiguity of natural language. A natural language requirements specification is overly flexible. You can say the same thing in completely different ways. It is up to the reader to find out when requirements are the same and when they are distinct.

There is no easy way to modularize natural language requirements. It may be difficult to find all related requirements. To discover the consequence of a change, you may have to look at every requirement rather than just a group of related requirements. Because of these problems, requirements specifications written in natural language are prone to misunderstandings. These are often not discovered until later phases of the software process. Then, they may be very expensive to resolve.

It is essential to write user requirements in a language that nonspecialists can understand. However, you can write system requirements in more specialized notations. These include stylized, structured natural language; graphical models of the requirements to use cases; or formal mathematical specifications.

Structured Language Specifications

Structured natural language is a way of writing system requirements where the freedom of the requirements writer is limited and all requirements are written in a standard way. This approach maintains most of the expressiveness and understandability of natural language, but it ensures that some degree of uniformity is imposed on the specification. Structured language notations limit the terminology that can be used. It uses templates to specify system requirements.

PM may incorporate control constructs derived from programming languages and graphical highlighting to partition the specification. One way is to use a form-based approach. To use a form-based approach to specify system requirements, you must define at least one standard form or template to express the requirements. The specification may be structured around the objects manipulated by the system, the functions performed by the system, or the events processed by the system. When a standard form is used for specifying functional requirements, the following information should be included:

- Description of the function or entity being specified
- Description of its inputs and where these come from
- Description of its outputs and where these go to
- Indication of what other entities are used (the requires part)
- Description of the action to be taken
- If a functional approach is used, a precondition setting out what must be true
- Before the function is called, a postcondition specifying what is true after the function is called
- Description of the side effects (if any) of the operation

Using formatted specifications removes some of the problems of natural language specification. Variability in the specification is reduced. Requirements are organized more effectively. However, it is difficult to write requirements in an unambiguous way, particularly when complex computations are required.

To address this problem, you can add extra information to natural language requirements using tables or graphical models of the system. These can show how computations proceed, how the system state changes, how users interact with the system, and how sequences of actions are performed. Tables are particularly useful when several possible alternative situations are available and you need to describe the actions to be taken for each of these.

Interface Specification

Almost all software systems must operate with existing systems that have already been implemented and installed in an environment. If the new and existing systems must work together, the interfaces of existing systems must be precisely specified. These specifications should be defined early in the process and included (perhaps as an appendix) in the requirements document. There are three types of interfaces:

- **Procedural interfaces:** Existing programs or subsystems offer a range of services that are accessed by calling interface procedures. These interfaces are sometimes called application programming interfaces (APIs).

- **Data structures:** These are passed from one subsystem to another. Graphical data models are the best notations for this type of description. If necessary, program descriptions in Java or C++ can be generated automatically from these descriptions.

- **Representations of data:** One of example is the ordering of bits. These have been established for an existing subsystem. These interfaces are most common in embedded, real-time systems. Some programming languages such as Ada (but not Java) support this level of specification. However, the best way to describe these is probably to use a diagram of the structure with annotations explaining the function of each group of bits.

Formal notations allow interfaces to be defined in an unambiguous way, but their specialized nature means they are not understandable without special training. They are rarely used in practice for interface specification. However, in my view, they are ideally suited for this purpose. A programming language like Java can be used to describe the syntax of the interface. However, this must be supplemented by further description, explaining the semantics of each of the defined operations.

Requirements: Gathering, Documentation, and Quality Assurance (QA)

In order to understand requirements gathering in iterative process, we need to understand some traditional processes used in requirements gathering. Since the satisfactory fulfillment of requirements is the core of this process, it is important to have a methodology for gathering and testing requirements.

Sources for Gathering Requirements

Requirements can come from a variety of sources:

- **Client:** This is the person or organization that pays for the development and will own the product. In our case, this is the United States Postal Service. An example of a requirement from the client might be that the software should be Y2K compliant.

- **Customer:** This is the person or organization that will buy the product from the client. For example, a customer may be a client's operations group. The operations group may have a requirement that your software must be compatible with another product they use.

- **End user:** This is the final consumer of a finished product. Different techniques are available to gather requirements from the end user, for example, interviews, prototyping, and usage scenarios. Usage scenarios capture the users' perspective in a narrative form, flow diagram, annotated screen shot, and/or other form. These techniques are particularly useful when the project involves automating an activity that the user manually performs.

- **Stakeholder:** This is anyone with a material interest in the project, including clients, customers, and users. An additional stakeholder might be, for example, the security office.

In this chapter, the terms "customer" and "user" are sometimes used interchangeably. These terms should be understood to include any stakeholder, that is, that person who ultimately thinks your product proves satisfactory.

Documenting Requirements

When gathering requirements, it is important to document them according to an agreed-upon standard. The standard we have chosen to follow is the Volere Requirements Specification Template. This standard is one of the most comprehended standards. It is divided into twenty-six sections. Each of which describes a certain type of requirement. For each requirement, we record the following information:

- **Requirement Number:** This number is of the form Rn.s, where n is the next unique requirement number and s is the section number described above for this type of requirement. For example, we gathered two requirements gathered so far from section 3 and section 7. The requirements would be numbered R1.3 and R2.7. Some of the template's sections are divided into subsections. For example, section 9a refers to functional requirements. Section 9b refers to data requirements. Thus, requirements for these two sections could be numbered R1.9a and R2.9b.

- **Description:** This is a brief statement of the requirement.

- **Customer Value:** This is the sum of the customer satisfaction rating and customer dissatisfaction rating. The customer satisfaction rating describes the degree of user satisfaction if the requirement is successfully implemented. The scale is from one (mild interest) to five (extremely critical). The customer dissatisfaction rating describes the degree of user dissatisfaction if the requirement is not successfully implemented. The scale is from one (hardly matters) to five (extremely displeased). For example, a requirement that is an absolute necessity to the user might be given a customer satisfaction rating of five (extremely critical and must be implemented) and a customer dissatisfaction rating of five (extremely displeased if not implemented) for a total customer value rating of ten. On the other hand, a requirement that was a "bell or whistle" might be given a customer satisfaction rating of four and a customer dissatisfaction rating of only one. The total customer value rating would be five. By prioritizing requirements on the basis of the customer value rating, the developers and customers can agree on which requirements will be implemented in a given iteration or project phase. Those requirements deemed less important may be saved for future releases or deleted altogether. The customer value rating can be especially useful when gathering requirements from disparate sources because it attempts to provide an objective method for prioritizing requirements based on what can be essentially subjective criteria.

- **Source:** This is the identity of the person who raised the requirement.

- **History:** This is the date the requirement was identified. It also includes its modifications and disposition.

Other information may be gathered about the requirements as the developers see fit.

#	Name	Description
1	Product Purpose	• The user problem or background to the project effort
2	Client, Customer, and Other Stakeholders	• The identity of all interested parties
3	Product Users	• A list of the potential users of the product and their characteristics
4	Requirements Constraints	• Constraints that have an effect on the product's requirements and design
5	System Terminology	• Definitions of all terms and acronyms used in the project

#	Name	Description
6	Relevant Facts	• External factors that have an effect on the product
7	Assumptions	• A list of the developers' assumptions
8	Product Scope	• The context of the work
9	Functional and Data Requirements	• Functions, data model, and fit criteria
10	Look and Feel Requirements	• Interface and style issues
11	Usability Requirements	• Ease of use and ease of learning issues
12	Performance Requirements	• Issues of speed, safety, precision, reliability, availability, and capacity
13	Operational Requirements	• Specifications of the expected physical and technological environment
14	Maintainability/ Portability Requirements	• Identify who will maintain the product • Describe the other platforms or environments to which the product will be ported
15	Security Requirements	• Confidentiality, file integrity, and audit issues
16	Cultural and Political Requirements	• Company policy, language, and acceptability issues
17	Legal Requirements	• Laws and standards with which the product must comply
18	Open Issues	• Issues that have been raised but not addressed or closed
19	Off-the-Shelf Solutions	• COTS products that could be bought • Reuse issues
20	New Problems	• A description of the problems the product could cause when implemented • Any limitations placed on the product by the implementation environment

#	Name	Description
21	Tasks	• A specification of the approach that will be taken • The development phases that will be necessary to deliver the product
22	Cutover	• Deployment activities
23	Risks	• A list of the most likely and most serious risks associated with the project
24	Costs	• A cost estimate for each deliverable
25	User Documentation	• List of documents that will be supplied as part of the product (including training documentation)
26	Waiting Room-	• Requirements that will not be implemented in the current phase of the project (might be implemented in a future release)

Table 7. Volere Requirements Specification Template.

Not all of these may apply to a given project.

Quality Assurance (QA)

Once IT and other sources have established the requirements, a QA process will aid in a well-managed implementation. The following are ten requirements tests that cover relevance, coherency, traceability, completeness, and other measures that address wrong, missing, vague, or incomplete requirements specifications. We will talk about implementation for this process later.

1. Does each requirement have a quality measure that can be used to test if any solution meets the requirement?

   • **Measurability:** Any solution that meets the measure is acceptable. Any solution that does not meet the measure is not acceptable.

   • **Quantifiability:** If the requirement states the system must perform its task quickly, that is not quantifiable. If the requirement states the system must perform its task within 60 seconds, that is quantifiable.

2. Does the specification contain a definition of the meaning of every essential subject matter term within the specification?

- **Coherency:** Word each requirement so it is not open to subjective interpretation.

3. Is every reference to a defined term consistent with its definition?

4. Is the context of the requirements wide enough to cover everything we need to understand?

   - **Completeness:** Avoid omitting requirements because we did not think of asking the right questions.

   - **Context:** Define the problem we are trying to solve. This includes all the requirements we eventually must meet, that is, anything we have to build or anything we have to change. Do not limit the focus to those parts of the system that will be automated. The solution may change how the users perform their jobs.

5. Have we asked the stakeholders about conscious, unconscious, and undreamed-of requirements? Can we show that a modeling effort has taken place to discover the unconscious requirements? Can we demonstrate that brainstorming or similar efforts have taken place to find the undreamed-of requirements?

   - **Conscious requirements:** These are problems that the new system must solve.

   - **Unconscious requirements:** These are problems that the current system already solved.

   - **Undreamed-of requirements:** This would be a requirement if we knew it was possible or could imagine it.

6. Is every requirement in the specification relevant to this system?

   - **Relevance:** Does a requirement contribute to the stated goals of the system? If this requirement is excluded, will it prevent us from achieving those goals?

7. Does the specification contain solutions posturing as requirements? If the requirement includes a piece of technology and another technology could implement it, then, unless the specified technology is a genuine constraint, the requirement is really a solution.

8. Is the stakeholder value defined for each requirement? Rate on a scale of one to five both the customer satisfaction (mild interest to very pleased if the requirement is implemented successfully) and the customer dissatisfaction (hardly matters to very displeased if the requirement is not met). The sum of the reward and penalty shows the overall value that a stakeholder places on a particular requirement.

9. Is each requirement uniquely identifiable?

    *   **Traceability:** Each requirement must have a unique identifier so we can show that our solution meets the requirement.

10. Is each requirement tagged to all parts of the system where it is used? For any change to requirements, can you identify all parts of the system where this change has an effect?

    *   **Event/use case:** This user-defined happening within the context of the system causes a preplanned response. The event/use case is a convenient way of grouping related requirements and tracing them through the development process.

The requirements specification must contain all the requirements that your product will implement. The customers, users, or other stakeholders communicate these requirements to the developers. Code is developed according to the requirements. The project is certified according to the requirements. In the end, the customer will accept the product based on the satisfactory implementation of the requirements.

With so many people involved with requirements during the life cycle of a project, it is important to specify objectively each requirement in a consistent manner. By using a consistent requirements methodology, you can minimize requirements-related defects.

This chapter illustrates one method for gathering requirements and then testing the quality of those requirements. During later stages of project development, testing will concentrate on the design and implementation of the solution using UML processes.

Team Development Case Process (TDCP)

This section addresses specific project development teams in the context of the respective development artifacts, including the component deliverables, for which the project teams are responsible, the tools used and formats applied in the development of these artifacts, and the traceabilities between these artifacts. The section itself provides a lightweight overview of the software engineering iterative development process for any COTS application. The team development case process (TDCP) is developed as a configuration, or customization, of the unified process. It should be adapted to the project's needs.

This portion is intended to be lightweight and introduce key traceability concepts of the RUP, as tailored for each COTS project, to the project staff without an overwhelming amount of detail. This short chapter does not capture the full set of RUP artifacts or drill down into the specific process workflow elements. Its purpose is to provide an introductory overview and associated definitions of what needs to be created per development phase. It is expected that project team members will refer, by artifact and/or *Wf,* to the associated online RUP project resources as necessary.

Component Deliverable Teams

The project focuses on several key disciplines:

- Project management is associated with a set of artifacts generated to manage the project and establish the working environment.
- Business modeling is associated with a set of artifacts generated to capture the business processes driving the software effort.
- Requirements are associated with a set of artifacts generated to define the system functionality to meet the business process and define testing criteria.
- Analysis and design is associated with a set of artifacts defining how the COTS components will be architected, configured, and deployed.
- Deployment is associated with a set of artifacts defining how the product will be deployed.
- Testing is associated with a set of artifacts for testing the constructed application.
- Courseware is associated with the congealing of artifacts from various artifact sets toward developing courseware-supported instruction solutions and associated artifacts.

The following maps these disciplines to their associated project teams:

Project Team	Discipline
Project Management Team	Project Management
Business Architecture Team	Business Modeling
Technical Architecture Team	Requirements
	Analysis and Design
Implementation Team	Deployment
Test Team	Testing
Training Team	Courseware Development

Table 8. Project teams and discipline.

The rest of this TDCP presents the following information associated with each of these project teams:

- Their purpose
- The artifact set produced and associated tool(s) and format(s) used
- The component deliverables, that is, key, larger-grained, and sometimes hierarchical deliverable artifacts for which the team is responsible
- Project traceability, that is, what aspects of artifact sets and related project deliverables are traceable to the next layer and how the traceability of the team's component deliverables map and are traceable to others

The following figure provides an artifact-oriented view of the workflow between the business architecture, technical architecture, configuration specification, and test and courseware teams. In this view, the partitions or swim lanes associated with each team contains artifacts, including component deliverables, for which the team is responsible.

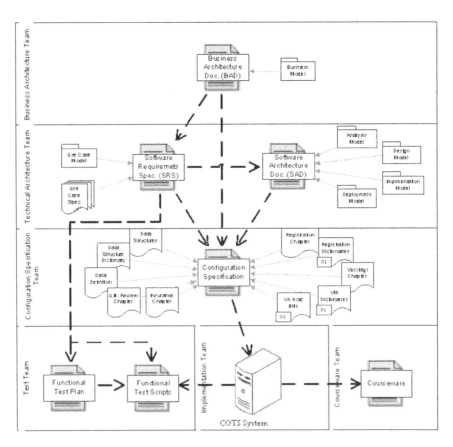

Figure 8. Component deliverable workflow (artifact-oriented).

The following figure provides an alternative, process-oriented view of the workflow between these same teams where the partitions or swim lanes associated with each team are focused on the business process activity that the team is responsible for performing. The respective artifacts are shown on the periphery of these activities. In this latter rendering, the volume component deliverables types, which are represented as documents, are shown on the transitions between activities and between teams. These component deliverables are indeed key artifacts that drive the workflow amongst these component development teams. The following sections further reinforce this point.

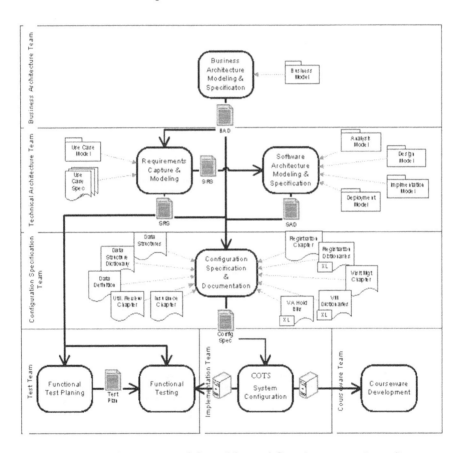

Figure 9. Component deliverable workflow (process-oriented).

Chapter Six

Project Management Office (PMO)

Project Management Office (PMO) Overview

For a long time, organizations completed projects on an as-needed basis. Management identified what needed to be done, determined which persons had the time, gathered the select few who were good developers, and pronounced them the newest team to create an application. At such time, someone from the group would be appointed as project manager and head of the team. Sometimes, these teams actually completed the projects. Most of the time, projects never completed. Managers would tell the team, "We need this done by this time. Here's how much time and funding you have." This sink-or-swim induction to project management is how many of us got started.

Experimentation with these processes eventually started the professional project management movement. The informal method slowly gave way to a new approach, that is, planning, management, and execution of prescribed tasks in a consistent and logical manner in order to ensure the successful completion of a project.

One of the success factors in today's project management is a solid process/methodology and an enforcement organization for keeping the project within the guidelines of that process. This is where the project management office (PMO) comes into the picture.

A PMO can be set up to function in two unique ways. In some organizations, a PMO consists of a program manager who will oversee multiple projects. All projects have their own respective project manager. The PMO acts as a governing body and connector for all the projects. On larger projects and, specifically, in large COTS implementation, the PMO acts as a support organization for the project manager. Because our focus in this book is iterative methodology and COTS implementation, we will be concentrating on this type of PMO setup.

Organizations delivering projects should have a unit that performs the management functions of the delivery process. There are many units within a project. Development creates the product. Test teams run the test scripts and log the defects. There is a need for management within these units to ensure smooth delivery of the product from its inception to client delivery. In the past few years, companies and organizations have realized that project management is a unique and essential discipline in success of the projects. The value of project management is measured either in a ROI or funds invested in project management functions. A PMO provides a starting point and governance structure for project management to ensure that projects stay within the guidelines of the methodology. It also acts as an information hub and direct support to the project manager.

When establishing a PMO, you need buy-in from all senior managers and stakeholders in the project, including the client. The project manger is ultimately responsible for successful delivery of the project. The PMO is the governance and enforcer of the process.

The PMO is a self-governing business that unites under the direction of the project manager. It enables the project manager to effectively manage the project by establishing processes and procedures, enforcing the rules, and controlling the project via tools that will be discussed later. The focus of the PMO is the development of management-accepted standards and practices that permit the repeated success of all iterations.

Not only should the PMO focus on the major project management processes, that is, project planning, building teams, execution, change control, and so forth, it must also formulate sound internal processes and fully satisfy the needs of external interfaces.

Develop Common Methods for Project Management

The PMO provides an organizational structure that supports the overall delivery process. It also develops common policies, processes, and standards that are its cornerstone. Every functional or system team lead follows the same process and procedures and develops the same type of reports in a standard format. Project communications are clear and presented in a manner that is consistent in content and structure. Finally, the PMO provides a point from which all aspects of the project can be evaluated. It clearly defines ownership and accountability for each section of the iteration. It establishes clear standards of performance measurement to judge the success of each component of iterations. Every team lead and group lead starts from here. They are held accountable to a common set of standards.

The PMO is a tactical asset for the project. This is where document management, configuration management (CM), essential project artifacts, and governance reside. Assigned team leads and group leads are focused on the daily coordination and management of teams. Thus, the PMO ensures good client relations.

The PMO provides daily monitoring and audit functions. Through reports and status reviews, it gives the project manager timely feedback about project goals, status, accomplishments, and issues. The PMO should be the source to which the project manager turns to assess a project's true status.

Not only does the PMO provide focus on delivery management, it also mentors less experienced group leads and encourages professional development in the discipline of project management. The exchange of information and professional experience among seasoned and developing group leads is an invaluable asset to any organization.

Communications

Communicating project status is critical. The PMO provides the central point from which all project statuses emanate. How this information is made available to senior management and project stakeholders must be detailed in the project communications plan. Project manager, the PMO, and staff must present a regular review of project status through scheduled reports, notices of critical issues, and formal presentations. Regardless of what tools you use, keep the following in mind when communicating project status:

- Tell it like it is. Never dress up bad news or even try to talk around it.

- Be factual. When you are giving the status, make sure you present all the facts correctly. This is especially true when reporting financial status of expediters and project controllers, projected expenses, and, if applicable, customer invoicing status.

- Be brief, concise, and to the point. Do not begin a long dissertation. Limit the number of charts you show when giving a project status review presentation. However, always have ready any charts that may help provide background information to address a particular question.

- Keep senior management updated on a regular basis. This helps curb their urge to micromanage the project. If you are a senior manager, I offer the following quote from Thomas Dreier, "When you find a man who knows his job and is willing to take responsibility, keep out of his way and don't bother him with unnecessary supervision. What you may think is cooperation is nothing but interference."

Finances

Controlling and managing project finances are not simple, but the PMO staff must not delegate that entire task back to the organization's accounting department. The PMO must have full authority and responsibility for the fiscal state of assigned project. This includes annotating man hours used to those estimated, authorizing purchases and associated expenses, invoicing, executing cost control measures, and financial reporting.

Procuring project items must be a short process. When project finances are split among several entities, this can result in the delayed purchase of items because one person has to approve the purchase, another has to log it, and a third has to send the procurement action. The PMO should authorize all purchases listed on approved project appropriation documents. There should be a direct interface to contract and procure in order to issue the purchase order. In addition, the PMO must provide for adjustments to a project's financial picture caused by scope changes, incorrect manpower, or financial estimates.

The PMO and financial unit are a team, so do not ignore your organization's accounting department. Provide it with project financial information, for example, expense and procurements authorized as well as projection of unused budget lines that remain obligated. Through the submission of accurate cash flow reports, the PMO must be able to project when expenses will be incurred. The PMO tracks project expenses. The accounting team takes the project financial data and folds it into the total corporate picture. More than likely, the accounting department is showing company financial data based on invoices paid for project items ordered or hours expended that will not be reported until the following month due to the payroll cycle. Therefore, the PMO should be the information point for project financial status because it has the most current picture in terms of funds spent.

Keeping track of project finances involves great attention to detail. Design and use spreadsheets with simple calculations and links or use commercial project tracking software to shrink that task to a manageable size.

Building Teams

The PMO builds the project team where every team lead or group lead provides the synergy for a successful project. Your PMO needs to establish a sound working relationship with team leads and group leads. Both the PMO and team leads have defined roles and responsibilities to each other.

Team leads can be considered to be contract providers. The PMO provides them with the equivalent to a RFP for an expected deliverable. The requirement document is developed with the participation of the functional unit when total program requirements are defined and specific deliverables are identified.

You need to get commitments to deliver from each affected team. The PMO relies on these commitments to prepare project plans, control timelines, and set customer expectations. Hold internal sources for deliverables accountable for meeting commitments … just as if they were third-party contractors.

If internal resources cannot be provided or if commitments cannot be met due to higher priority tasking, then the PMO must be told so it can acquire external resources and address subsequent funding issues. Provisioning internal resources can often conflict with senior management's desire to maintain an economical staffing level. That conflict can place strain on meeting the resource needs of the PMO.

In the end, once the corporate commitment to deliver a product or service to a customer is made and expectations are set, everyone must manage his respective area to meet that commitment. From executive management to the project team and supporting technical staff, no one is off the hook.

Customer Management

The PMO organization, standards, and execution of the delivery process must ultimately focus on the customer. No matter how well the project is planned or management process is executed or how good the product quality is, the project fails if customer expectations are not fulfilled.

By involving the customer from the outset as part of the project team rather than a sideline bystander, you set the needed positive tone. Make your customer part of the project plan development and planning process. You both must agree from the start what to provide, when, and at what cost. Once you have established this baseline, your focus turns to customer relations and management.

Project Management Processes

One of the foundations of building and maintaining customer confidence is having your customer understand the delivery management process you follow. During the discovery phase of the project, a team of your sales and PMO staff should show the customer the product or service to be delivered as well as demonstrate how your company will manage delivery on time and on budget.

Develop the project plan so it specifies to both sides, that is, project team and customer, how the project will be managed to final delivery. The more detail that goes into the project plan, the more informed all recipients are. All iterations should be defined based on the application functions.

After the project plan has been developed, hold two kickoff meetings. Meet once with the internal project team. The other time, meet with the customer and their principals at the customer location. Make sure that all team members understand the change management process from the beginning.

Regularly meeting with the users is beneficial. After the initial kickoff meeting, it helps to hold regularly scheduled meetings with the customer stakeholders at their location. These meetings limit the time that customers must take from their schedules, display the willingness of your company to go the extra length, and foster building of relationships between the PMO, project manager, and customer. Meetings also provide both the customer and PMO principal an opportunity to physically review any site preparation activities that may be part of the project.

Some of the tools for project management process management include defect management process, change control process, configuration management process, risk management process, code promotion process, and project timeline.

Any large project must invest in establishing a PMO to manage the delivery of products. When sufficiently staffed and equipped with up-to-date technical resources, the PMO can be a powerful asset for the organization, ensuring team cooperation and providing the highest standards of user care while delivering services and products on time and on budget.

Principles of Sound Documentation

One of the functions of the PMO is to be the central location for documentation. In order to ensure consistency within documents, the PMO is chartered to ensure standards in documentation across projects. The next section describes the process of creating such consisted documentation and process.

The project documentation process follows the seven principles of documentation. These principles provide the foundation for our documentation process.

- **Write from the reader's viewpoint:** A document is only read if it meets the needs of its intended audience. Material that is written in streams of consciousness or uses arcane terminology is unlikely to meet the reader's needs. Thus, it is unlikely to be read or consulted often.

- **Avoid unnecessary repetition:** While repetition sometimes reinforces a point, its use in technical information becomes troublesome over time. Repetition is the root of inconsistency. Keeping track of all repeats is difficult, if not impossible. Thus, repeated information becomes inconsistent over time. Attempts to avoid these inconsistencies are costly.

- **Avoid ambiguity:** This principle might better be stated as "avoid unintended ambiguity." Software documents are, by nature, ambiguous in areas that remain undecided until the system is implemented. Nevertheless, if a decision is made, the documentation must communicate it unambiguously so that system stakeholders do not misinterpret it. Such misinterpretation can lead to confusion, incorrect implementation, or problems during system verification and validation.

- **Use a standard organization:** Usually, a document is not read more than once, if that. Yet, if it is successful, readers will refer to it numerous times. Providing a standard organization helps a reader quickly find information as well as provides the architect with guidance on what needs to be captured and what has or has not been captured at any given time.

- **Record rationale:** The reasoning behind the decisions is just as important as the decisions themselves. Documentation lives with the system. As most developers have experienced, the reasoning behind a decision may be forgotten in as little as a few weeks. Understanding the rationale behind decisions helps the architect refrain from revisiting decisions, helps designers understand why specific choices were made, and supports system evolution by stating explicitly that certain decisions were based on the context and technological constraints imposed at the time.

- **Keep documentation current but not too current:** While documentation should not become out-of-date, disseminating recent modifications to certain team members may be ill-advised at times. Documentation remains the final authority. Stakeholders consult it for guidance when making decisions about the system. Including information that might not be final does not help them. Organizations are well-advised to determine a documentation release plan that is appropriate to their practices and processes.

- **Review documentation for fitness of purpose:** Documentation is successful only if it meets its readers' needs. Thus, these readers determine its usefulness. They should be encouraged to provide feedback if this does indeed happen.

In the coming section about portals, there will be detailed discussion on how portals are specifically designed to support the document process in following the principles discussed previously.

Document Types

In COTS implementations and software development projects that follow the iterative process, seven main documents need to be considered.

1. A software architecture document (SAD) is a crucial facet in the development of a software system. But it is often carried out in a haphazard fashion, if at

all. Lack of attention to the documentation results from insufficient guidance about what should be documented and when and how the information should be captured so that project teams find it useful. A system is envisioned that enables the architect to capture architectural decisions and related artifacts as a living repository that can communicate information to project team, who might be both geographically and temporally distributed. The system must communicate in a way that allows each project team quick and easy access to information that is relevant to the person's role in the software development process. Documenting software architecture is a matter of describing the appropriate architectural views and then adding information that applies to more than one view. Architectural views represent different software perspectives that support the varying needs of the project team. In this approach, perspectives are categorized as view types, which are specialized by styles, that provide the guidance for creating a view.

- **View types:** In our approach, three types of views provide the foundation for structuring architecture documentation: module, component-and-connector, and allocation. A view type is defined in terms of a set of element types and relation types. For instance, the elements of the module view type are modules, that is, principle implementation units of the software. Relation types describe how the modules are related to each other. Each element and relation type may have associated properties that are also described as part of the view type's definition.

- **Styles:** In a view type, patterns of interactions often occur that can be captured as styles, or patterns, that provide architectural solutions based on quality requirements and other software concerns. Architectural styles may refine element and relation types. In addition, they may include a set of constraints on the interactions. For example, the module view type includes the decomposition style, which focuses on how system responsibilities are spread across the implementation units and how the modules are decomposed into submodules. This style is based on the is-part-of relation and includes constraints specifying the decomposition graph may not contain loops and no module may be part of more than one module in a view. While the book describes several styles associated with each view type, these styles are not intended to be all-encompassing. The system architect remains free to define or adopt styles from other systems when appropriate. When a style is created or adopted, the architect must define it within the architecture documentation.

- **Views:** When the architectural styles are determined, the architect constructs views on the software to support the stakeholders' needs. Views describe some aspect of the system in terms of system-specific elements and relations. Relations are defined in terms of the element and the style's relation types and submit to the constraints that the style imposes.

2. The software requirements specification (SRS) is the official statement of what the system developers should implement. It should include both the user requirements for a system and a detailed specification of the system requirements. In some cases, the user and system requirements may be integrated into a single description. In other cases, the user requirements are defined in an introduction to the SRS. If there are a large number of requirements, the detailed system requirements may be presented in a separate document. The requirements document has a diverse set of users, ranging from the senior management of the organization who are paying for the system to the engineers who are developing the software. The diversity of possible users means the requirements document must be a compromise between communicating the requirements to customers, defining the requirements in precise detail for developers and testers, and including information about possible system evolution. Information on anticipated changes can help system designers avoid restrictive design decisions and help system maintenance engineers who must adapt the system to new requirements. The level of detail you should include in a requirements document depends on the type of system that is being developed and the development process used. When an external contractor will develop the system, critical system specifications need to be precise and very detailed. When there is more flexibility in the requirements and where an in-house, iterative development process is used, the requirements document can be much less detailed. Any ambiguities can be resolved during development of the system. As a standard in the industry, we suggest the following structure for SRS documents:

Introduction	• Purpose of the requirements document • Scope of the product • Definitions, acronyms, and abbreviations • References • Overview of the remainder of the document
General description	• Product perspective • Product functions • User characteristics • General constraints • Assumptions and dependencies

Specific requirements	• Cover functional, nonfunctional, and interface requirements

Table 9. SRS document structure.

The specific requirements are obviously the most substantial part of the document. Because of the wide variability in organizational practice, it is not appropriate to define a standard structure for this section. The requirements may document external interfaces, describe system functionality and performance, as well as specify logical database requirements, design constraints, emergent system properties and quality characteristics.

3. The data structure/definition generally outlines the relationship between all data elements within each iteration and the project as a whole. With each iteration, this document gets updated and moves horizontally. We will discuss the use of this document in detail during the iteration process. We have talked in detail about this document in the system/business architecture process in chapter four. For now, please keep in mind that this of one of the essential documents for each iteration.

4. A functional test plan (FTP), or unit test plan, is a document that is generated in each iteration. We have discussed this document as part of overall testing process in the test chapter. This document outlines the testing process with each iteration. FTP only considers the functions in each individual iteration. It is not intended for business verification.

5. The information in the business requirements document (BRD) is essential to gather during the requirements gathering process. This document was discussed in the requirements chapter.

6. The business architecture document (BAD) will enable the business process to look at each process within the iteration and understand the relationship between business process and the functions of that iteration. For the process of creating this document, please refer to the business modeling process chapter.

7. The courseware documents could be the most important documents that are created during the iteration. You can create the best system in the world, but, if your users do not possess the knowledge to use the system, you project will fail. In each iteration, you will create the courseware for the prior iteration. We talk about the courseware creation in detail during the training section

Document Process

The goal of this process is to give the team access to work on component documents from a collaboration site, understand the annotation process and the staging process for daily/weekly publication of documents.

Business Roles

The primary roles are:

- **Component lead:** Team member responsible for a set of documents
- **Component team:** Team involved in creating and editing documents
- **Document owner:** Member of the component team, but not the component lead
- **Documentation team:** Team responsible for document management and grammatical quality
- **Defect owner:** Team member responsible for the resolution of a logged defect
- **Reviewer:** Customer/project staff responsible for reviewing system documentation
- **QAD team:** Team responsible for weekly review of documents
- **QA lead:** Team member responsible for facilitating the QAD

Preconditions

The precondition for this process is that the components are available for review. The following figure provides the flow of events that will describe the document life cycle.

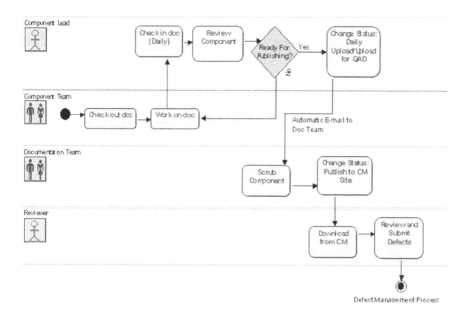

Figure 10. Flow of events.

Publishing Site for Iterations

A publishing site for each iteration is available on the portal. Each site consists of a set of workspaces, each referenced by a list of document owners and their assigned documents. Within each workspace are document libraries containing a copy of the namesake component/document, weekly defect reports, and other associated documents that are part of the ongoing iteration management and review of iteration components.

Each workspace on the site also contains a document tracking area. Here, documents are staged for publication. The users of this site do not have delete rights.

The Document Workspace (Component Team)

On an as-needed basis, the component lead and component team will actively edit and collaborate on the documents in a document workspace. To get to the document workspace for a component, users must click the appropriate title. Each document will have a listing that will allow the document owner to check in and check out the document for updating, revising, defect resolution, and so forth. Each of the document workspaces will have versioning turned on so the component lead can review changes that have occurred over time.

The site can be accessed via a team link on the home page of the SharePoint portal, Team Workspaces. The link is only visible to team member, and it will take team members to the collaboration site.

Daily Document Management

Each component lead ensures that his or her component, including chapters, appendices, and so forth, is up-to-date and individual documents are checked in by close of each business day every workday. This includes once per weekday and once per weekend and holidays as necessary. This refresh will ensure the work done on the document is captured on the portal, minimizing the risk of losing critical updates.

Document Promotion (Component Lead, Documentation Team)

When a component lead/document lead determines the assigned documents have been revised as required to reflect defect fixes, as soon as possible each day, he or she will click the document title in the document tracking area of the workspace and click Edit Item from the top navigation. He or she will change the status of the document to Daily Upload or Upload for QAD as appropriate. Then he or she will click Save and Close. This will trigger a system e-mail to the documentation team, indicating the document is available for upload and editing.

During the following two hours or until the document tracking status indicates it is published, the documentation team will edit the document to correct obvious grammatical and spelling errors. Then the team will publish it to the site. Document owners must not attempt to check out, download, or modify their documents during the uploading process. Continuing to work on the document after it is staged for upload will cause you to lose any edits that the documentation team applied to the version that was uploaded for public viewing.

After a document has been published to the collaboration site, the documentation team will change the status of the document to be published in the document tracking area. The documentation team will publish documents daily, except weekends and holidays.

Document and Defect Annotation (Component Team)

The component lead/document owner must flag any changes to the document, whether in response to a logged defect rated higher than cosmetic or new content that is added between QAD review meetings, by inserting a comment into the document. If the new content is in response to a defect, the writer must reference the defect tracking system defect number.

QAD Weekly Review (QAD Team)

A team of reviewers consisting of project team members, customers, and business unit will be designated to review each component weekly. Each team will be assigned a QA lead. Reviewers will follow the PMO defect process for submitting, assigning, resolving, and closing defects. To stage an upload of documents for the weekly QAD, refer to "Document Promotion."

The document owners must submit all documents for their components no later than 11:00 AM each Wednesday. The documentation team will review each document for grammatical and spelling errors and upload the documents to the collaboration site in the relevant iteration tab. The documentation team will send an e-mail to the review team with a link to the collaboration site, including the most current documents available for the weekly defect review process. As of noon on Wednesday, the notice to reviewers will also provide a report for open and closed defects for each component.

Update Document (Component Team)

After each review cycle, the component team updates and revises documents in the collaboration site. At the end of the review period, the component lead and documentation team repeat this process until the component is locked for the current iteration. Once the component is locked, the documentation team will modify the collaboration site and workspace to remove unneeded access rights from current document leads and contributors. The documentation team will then assign appropriate rights to the component lead and contributors for the next iteration.

Daily Defect Update (Reviewers and Component Team)

Because documents are staged daily for public viewing, the customer and project team members will have continuous access to component documentation and will be able to submit defects via a defect system. The component team must revise documentation in response to any critical defects submitted on a daily basis. The component team follows the process outlined in "Document Promotion" to update the documents.

Fields

The following are some of the important fields in the document tracking area of the workspaces:

Name	Default Value	Purpose
Send E-mail	Yes	• If yes, sends e-mail while saving row
Assigned to	Name of Document Owner	• Identifies individuals who can modify the document and authorize its publishing.
Cc	Document Editor	• Sends copy to document team, who is always copied on e-mail • May include others
Status	See list below	• State and/or action request
Workspace	Name of Workspace	• Identifies sender and document space where the e-mail was generated

Table 10. Status field values.

Value	Default	Purpose
Requested	Yes	• Document not on workspace • Please add an entry
Published		• Owner can start or resume work on document
Upload Daily		• Ready for daily upload
Upload to QAD		• Ready for weekly upload
Requires Attention		• There is a problem
Completed		• This record is not used anymore

Table 11.

The system maintains the start and due dates will facilitate tracking. A history field maintains an audit trail on this site.

Chapter Seven

Process Documentation

Integrated Portal Technologies

Your project's portal is among the most important tools of project management. Portals have significant potential to transform how projects do work and conduct business. Using portals, projects can streamline processes and transactions, increase employee productivity, and strengthen relationships with customers and partners.

This chapter discusses the scope of the broad portal challenge. It identifies capabilities to plan for, evaluates technologies to employ, and reviews the impact your technical choices will have on your project.

Portal

The term "portal" describes a wide variety of Web sites, ranging from internal sites for employees (Intranet) to external sites aimed at consumers and partners (Internet or extranet). In general terms, a portal is a Web site that aggregates contextually relevant information, applications, and services. A portal distills the complexity and variety of information and services available to a user into a single interface that is targeted to that user's needs and interests. Portals are a direct response to the breadth and complexity of the online world and the need for collaboration.

The goal of a portal is to simplify access to disparate resources throughout the project. Project-facing portals generally offer some combination of collaboration functionality and application integration. That is, Intranet portals provide and control access to the information and collaborative environments that employees need to do their jobs as well as provide a unified interface for interacting with multiple lines of business systems. Intranet portals are fast becoming critically important because they allow team members to find and collect relevant information, collaborate with great efficiency, and make new connections between disparate information sources and applications.

In this chapter, we will discuss the capabilities that a good project portal should have, regardless of which portal software providers or technology each would use. In general, you should select a tool that you and your team are familiar with and have the management and development capabilities. For example, you should not use a tool that relies heavily on Java coding capabilities if you do not have any Java developers on your team.

Portal Capabilities

As you review your portal frameworks, you should understand the breadth of capabilities required to meet all potential portal requirements. This can help define what your technical needs are today. It can also help you plan for future needs and reveal where your greatest challenges might lie. A review of key portal scenarios shows the most commonly required capabilities fall into the following broad categories: user authentication, personalization, application integration and aggregation, search, collaboration, Web content management, workflow, and analytics. These capabilities and their technical implications are discussed in the following sections.

User Authentication

By definition, portals imply content and functionality that is tailored to individual users. First, identify the users accessing the portal. For some portal applications, such as Web storefronts, this may be accomplished through weak user identification, for example, cookies. However, for other portals, especially Intranet portals, user authentication must be stronger, requiring secure user IDs and passwords.

Authentication can cause problems, especially if each system on the portal requires its own user ID and password. The key to keeping a portal usable is for the users to authenticate themselves once when signing on to the portal or system. Then they can have access to all content and functionality that the portal offers. This is known as single sign-on (SSO). This requires that the various components aggregated on the portal use or integrate with the same network authentication scheme.

Personalization

Personalization describes the process where different content can be presented to a user based on who they are, where they are located on the portal, or even how they have interacted with the portal in the past. A portal can be personalized in two basic ways:

- **Presentation of information, or interface personalization:** Users can customize specific parts of the user interface, for example, determining which pieces of content appear where, picking different display styles, selecting services and back-end systems to be displayed, and so forth.

- **Content and functionality, or content targeting:** Which content a user sees is often a blend of user preferences and choices that the underlying application made automatically. These system choices are based on business logic, for example, user profile (employee versus partner) or past purchasing or browsing behavior.

These two modes of personalization generally require two different approaches. Interface personalization requires a database of user profiles and a Web site rendering engine that business logic processing directs. Content targeting requires deeper analysis, often called analytics, where data mining and user segmentation inform the complex business logic that determines what is rendered.

Application Integration

Application integration is the connection of separate systems through data sharing and automated transactions. Enterprise application integration (EAI) can connect the test management system, for example, with the test reporting applications. Though these applications may not need to integrate directly with each other in a portal implementation, they will likely need to communicate, that is, expose data and functionality, to the portal itself, as it provides a single interface to multiple applications and content sources.

Again, a common framework helps simplify the problem. For instance, SSO technologies can ease setting access to different data sources and applications. If a user's profile does not allow access to particular data, then the portal should not offer access to that user.

Content Aggregation

Content aggregation expands on the key notion of creating content once and reusing it in multiple locations. Content aggregation involves gathering content from disparate sources and then displaying that content within a single interface, that is, the portal. Using content aggregation capabilities, a portal can present a unified view of content that may have different owners, hail from different project locations, or reside in different systems.

Content aggregation can be accomplished using content management technologies. Because portals themselves require significant content management functionality, as discussed later, there are benefits to centralizing on a single content management system, even if your content is dispersed across several different databases and servers.

Search

Search is an essential element of all portals, particularly content-driven portals, because it enables users to find exactly what they are looking for, regardless of whether or not the resource they need to access is intuitively categorized within the portal's navigational structure or taxonomy.

The simplest search implementation allows free text searches of a set of documents, Web sites, or other content. Search tools will usually include the ability to conduct parameterized searches against any metadata that has been captured with, or is implicit to, documents on the portal. For example, you may want to search for all documents that a certain individual wrote or all documents categorized with a specific keyword. More complex implementations enable searches of assets in content management systems as well as searches through the actual content of a wide variety of file types, for example, PDFs or database records.

At the same time, search functionality must also work with user profiles and security settings so users conducting searches only see results for assets to which they have access. Searches may also use rich information in a user profile to further refine and personalize search criteria.

Again, tight integration between capabilities helps reduce cost, time, and risk. Content management and personalization applications must work together to provide effective search capability.

Collaboration

Collaboration is another broad capability associated with portals. Collaboration features such as meeting spaces, project sites, workflow, document posting and versioning, check-in/checkout, discussion groups, real-time communication (chat), polls, subscriptions, and customizable alerts enable knowledge workers to effectively combine their efforts. Collaboration capabilities enable people to work together both synchronously and asynchronously.

Again, tight integration with other capabilities helps lower cost and risk. For example, collaboration tools integrated with productivity applications and search tools enable knowledge workers to find the information they need to make decisions as well as record those decisions in documents. Then they can share and collaborate on those documents with co-workers within a single, seamless portal environment that requires minimal IT intervention to create, maintain, and modify.

Web Content Management (WCM)

Content management refers to the capacity to store, manage, and cross-reference documents of all kinds. As such, content management is an essential aspect of data-centric portals. Web content management (WCM) focuses on the capability of authoring, storing, managing, and publishing content to the Web. Web-based content may include HTML pages, Active Server Pages (ASP) pages, images, sound clips, XML files, plain text, and rich media. It may also include other ancillary content such as style sheets and metadata.

Despite the traditional aggregation role of portals, the ability to create and manage unique, Web-based content on the portal is increasingly seen as an essential capability. For example, the project's Intranet site may primarily provide access to line of business systems. But it could also use WCM capabilities to enable publishing of internal, breaking news stories from the project communication team. Furthermore, the WCM system could also be used to aggregate press releases posted on the company Intranet site as it pertains to the project into a comprehensive project news section of the Intranet portal.

One of the key services WCM provides is empowering business users to take control over their own content. A sophisticated content management system can relieve Web administrators from the day-to-day publishing of content to the portal. Instead, business analysts are able to work within the WCM system to handle content creation, approval, and publishing tasks on their own.

A solid WCM system, closely integrated with other parts of the portal, such as user authentication, personalization, and search, can add significant value to a portal deployment.

Workflow

In the context of portals, workflow is primarily the process that controls how content is approved and published. Workflow is enables the project team to control content because it limits approval and publishing rights based on criteria that the PMO and project management team determine. Sophisticated workflow includes alert functions to notify the next approver that content is ready for them to review, customizable approval paths to enable parallel processing, and variable review levels for different categories of content. Workflow can also form an essential part of a collaboration portal, where, for example, multiple parties have to sign off on group work before it is submitted as final.

Other workflow requirements are more transaction-oriented. For example, this could include using project rules to define how a requirement is handled once it is submitted to the PMO via the portal.

Regardless of the context, workflow must be easy to access for business users. Preferably, it should integrate status reporting and notifications within the tools they already use to do work. Workflow must also be easy to customize and extend for technical workers designing solutions that span multiple systems and scenarios.

Analytics and Reporting

Online business analytics provide the project with information to optimize its effectiveness. In a large project, you can generate gigabytes of data and reports such as status reports, change management, and so forth. The PMO must organize and manage this immense amount of work. Analytics and reporting helps the project manager make intelligent project decisions. It will also create a window into the project for senior management and project sponsors. In this aspect, a good portal setup will contain all project information by accessing the data in real time from all other project systems.

Architecture for Portals

In addition to these basic capabilities, an integrated approach to portals requires some common architectural elements, including a rendering framework and common development and test environments.

Rendering Framework

The rendering framework is the server technology that is responsible for assembling and rendering a Web site. In most cases, modern application server architecture enable developers to work with abstracted notions of Web sites and remain shielded from writing HTML.

Portals tend to be made up of several different pieces brought together. Therefore, a good rendering framework will have ready-made elements that can radically reduce development time. Because the rendering framework must interoperate with all the other parts of the portal system, including the WCM system, personalization system, and collaboration system, there is significant benefit to having them access a common Web rendering technology. This will eliminate the need for higher cost development resources to maintain your portal.

Common Development Environment

Creating and deploying portals can be as simple as enabling a team site service on a file server or using public folders in Microsoft Outlook. In large projects, portals are complex development projects that require integration of several technologies. Then they require development of custom functionality on top of those integrations. This complexity is especially evident as the lines between the project team section of the portal and client-facing parts of the portal blur and the project demands for more sophisticated functionality increase.

Given these conditions, there is significant benefit in working with an integrated stack of portal technologies as well as a single development environment that is compatible across that entire stack of technology. If that development environment is easy to use, directly integrates with the portal technologies, and leverages common skill sets within your team, your portal development process can be much faster and less expensive.

Available Products

Several technology products are available in the market today, including IBM WebSphere, Oracle Portal, and Microsoft SharePoint.

Iterative Portal Solution Scenario

In the previous section, we discussed Web portals and their capabilities in a general sense. In the following section, we will discuss a portal solution scenario that will provide a sampling of typical portal implementation in an iterative environment. We will also discuss the essential capabilities that an iterative portal should posses in order to become an effective tool.

Project Portal

Iterative projects require cooperation among team members and continual communication. This scenario addresses the critical need for iteration project team members to share important information and ideas and collaborate on project documents. (See the previous chapter for details on the document promotion process.)

Capabilities

In an iterative project, your portal should cover some critical functions:

- Search is the ability to search for documents. It also includes the ability to use a global taxonomy as well as search for and categorize locally created and aggregated content.

- Collaboration is the ability to store current and archived documents in a common place; check documents in and out; categorize documents and attach metadata; interact with other knowledge workers through chat, e-mail, and so forth. It also includes the ability to take polls; host public discussions; aggregate or syndicate content from multiple, heterogeneous sources inside and outside of the enterprise into a single, consistent format; and cache aggregated content in a local content repository.

- Workflow is the ability to route and approve documents. Once implemented, the portal essentially replaces the combination of systems that project teams would typically use to communicate and share pertinent project information. Instead of working through multiple systems, team members can access functionality such as collaboration, storage, public folders, and spreadsheet-based lists on the team's Web workspace.

- WCM is the ability for a select group of employees to author HTML-based content in any language. It is also the ability for Web designers and IT staff to create templates to enforce consistent branding and presentation.

- Reporting is the ability to create and post reports from various systems.

- Business service aggregation is prebuilt integration components and the ability to write new integrations.

- Personalization is the ability for authors to personalize content for specific employees, that is, senior management and stakeholders.

Solution

Each iteration team generally uses the project team workflow section of the collaboration portal in a decentralized manner. The effectiveness of iteration teams is tied to their ability to efficiently create, store, find, and revise content among their team. Documents are usually at the heart of the project team collaboration portal. A typical business document will have a life cycle that involves conception, creation, distribution, discussion, revision, repurposing, and, finally approval. The nature of the document will dictate how much or how little it participates in each of those processes, but all documents will participate in these steps to some degree.

By using the right portal technologies, you can integrate document collaboration features directly into your document tool set. The integrated features enable team members to see who has contributed to a document, initiate real-time communications with other team members, and check required documents in and out of the repository. The communication portion of the project collaboration portal will focus on delivering relevant information and applications to project as well as client teams. Most typically, a small number of authors in a communication team publish content. A large audience then consumes it. Such structured publisher and project team roles will likely necessitate an authorization workflow to approve content before posting. Of course, not all content will be developed exclusively for the portal. Some content may be syndicated or aggregated from other sources, such as team or client portals.

Because the communication portion of the portal typically contain large amounts of content, personalization can improve communication by enabling users to organize their interface to highlight content most relevant to them. Personalization tools allow them to define view preferences and locate pertinent information quickly and easily.

The project portal is an important part of any project because it can help to lower costs, increase team productivity, control documentation, and strengthen relationships with clients and partners. The project portal pulls together data and functionality from disparate sources into an accessible package that is tailored to the needs of the individual team member.

Initially, portals were viewed as discreet, stand-alone deployments. Each had a single purpose. Today, the volume and complexity of portal deployments as well as the pervasive project need for increased agility are compelling project teams to take a broader approach to addressing portal requirements.

Chapter Eight

Pretesting Methodologies

Introduction

It is said that salespeople always say yes and project managers always say no. This is true in a sense that, as a project manager, you do not want to change your scope. Scope change means chaos and unpredictability. But that should not always be the case. As a client-facing project manager, you do not have the option of saying no most of the time. It is seen as pure stonewalling. You are not prepared to be cooperative or, worse, your team just is not competent. Either can cause you serious problems in your sponsor relationship, which maintaining is one of your top priorities. You have to come across as a diplomat that listens to the client needs, even if it means changing the scope.

Balancing between saying no to changes and accepting all proposed changes and causing major project control problems is a tough act. By using the iterative process, you have some flexibility, but you are still adding work. Using a well-defined change control process helps the stakeholder understand the effects of the requested change. One of the core, unbreakable rules of project management is that every project, no matter the size or methodology used, needs a change control process.

In this section, we will discuss the process of change control and how you should run a change control board (CCB). Change control is a formal process since the requirements documents and statement of work (SOW) are legal and contractually binding documents. Any changes to either one of these documents should be a formal process in writing. At the end of the project, the whole system is verified and tested against the requirements and changes through a change control process. As mentioned before, every project contains changes. Without a formal written change control process, your requirements documents will not be true representation of the delivered product.

Integrated Change Control Process

Integrated change control is defined as the management of change across the project in a single process group. Some of its purpose is to influence the causes of change, determine if a change is needed or has occurred, and manage the resulting approved change. This process includes scope, schedule, quality, and configuration management. The general assumptions in the change control process in all projects are as follows:

- Anyone on the project team can initiate a change request.
- The CCB must approve a change request before it is officially part of the project.
- The integrated change control processes will be used to execute all changes within its defined scope of control.
- No change that would normally be expected to adhere to the integrated change control process will occur outside of that process, such as direct agreements among project team members.
- A change can impact any of a number of areas of the project, the most common being categorized as project-level change, including schedule, scope, quality, and configuration modifications that are characteristic of a process flow, algorithm, screen, or other items. These other items may include cost impact as well as administrative approaches/processes, documents/deliverables/artifacts, and other non-product-related items.

Exceptions to the assumptions include the following:

- A group working on a project deliverable or artifact will regularly modify language, context, and format prior to its acceptance. These changes will not be required to adhere to the integrated change control process unless those changes impact schedule, scope, quality, or another approved deliverable/artifact.
- Immaterial modifications, including spelling, grammar, format corrections, and so forth, to approved deliverables/artifacts will not be required to adhere to the integrated change control process.

Change Control Board (CCB) Review Requirements

The CCB must review all changes that have a possible impact to project scope, schedule, quality, or cost.

Configuration Management Review Requirements

The defect review team (DRT) must review all changes that have a possible modification to approved/controlled deliverable, artifact, process, functionality, performance, acceptance criteria, quality requirements, documentation, plans other than project schedule, or configuration items.

Configuration Management Process

Upon submission into the configuration management process, change and defect requests are synonymous from the configuration management perspective. During this process, the DRT evaluates the change or defect request. The request will be specified as a change request or defect request. A defect request will be assigned to the configuration management change process. A change request will be assigned back to the change management process that is approved for project-level changes.

At his or her discretion, the project manager may determine an emergency change is needed. The project manager may approve this change at any time. The project manager is then responsible for reporting the following to the CCB: reason for emergency change, actions taken, and impact of change.

Primary Goals of the Integrated Change Control Process

The primary goals of the integrated change control process include the following:

- Manage change requests for the purpose of balancing scope, schedule, cost, functionality, quality, performance, and documentation throughout the life of the project
- Determine impact of changes prior to their approval
- Incorporate change only with the approval of the CCB
- Gain agreement for change among all project partners
- Provide appropriate level of documentation for change

Benefits of an Integrated Change Control

The benefits of an integrated change control include the following:

- Introducing change into the project environment in a logical, orderly, and timely fashion

- Reducing the negative impact of changes, minimizing the disruption of change, and addressing some of the root causes of project failures, including scope creep, budget creep, and schedule expansion
- Understanding the impact of implementing change
- Enabling project management to compile a snapshot of current activities and assess, at any time, the business, technical, project, and product impact of change, thus enhancing management's ability to make appropriate decisions based on current and planned activities
- Setting expectations of stakeholders by identifying impacts of changes prior to their implementation

Change Control Board (CCB)

In order to control the scope of the project, you should have a good change control process. In the following sections we will discuss the process for setting up a CCB board and the procedures that will govern the CCB meeting process. The CCB meeting should be a formal process for the following reasons:

- The formality and impact analysis will enable stakeholders and project sponsors to understand the impact of their decision.
- Formal approval of changes that have budget and time impacts allows for changes in the timeline and budget of the project and ensures proper approval and communications.
- It encourages open discussion on each change so other systems involved in the project notice the impacts of the change.

CCB Meeting Process

Each CCB meeting will begin with a roll call of all participants. CCB meeting quorum should include the following people: all project stakeholders, project sponsor, representative from all systems involved in the project with approval authority, representative from finance with budget approval authority, and project manager.

A quorum is a required set of individuals from each stakeholder, must be established for the CCB meeting to begin. The required participant may designate a proxy for representation at the CCB meeting. However, the proxy must be designated in writing to the CCB meeting facilitator.

If a quorum has not been established within ten minutes after the scheduled start time, then the meeting will be cancelled. There will be no exceptions. Change requests will not be discussed.

The CCB meeting will be separated into two distinct sections: discussion of new changes and approval of changes. The context of the first section of the meeting will be to discuss selected new change requests. The context of the second section of the meeting will be to vote on change requests discussed at the prior CCB meeting. This will allow sufficient time for each impacted system and stakeholder to analyze the impact. The discussion and vote for the same change request will not occur within an individual CCB meeting.

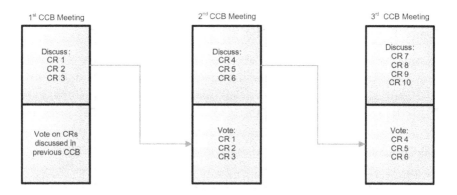

Figure 11. CCB meeting procedure.

Discussion of a Change Request

Based on the following criteria, a change request will be incorporated into the discussion section of the CCB meeting:

- The change request must be entered in time prior to the CCB meeting.

- An e-mail will be generated and sent to all stakeholders to identify the change requests for which discussion and voting is necessary. The e-mail will be distributed by end of business day of the day prior to the CCB meeting.

- The owner of a change request is required at the CCB meeting to discuss the change request. If the owner is unable to attend, he or she may provide a proxy.

- After the discussion of a change request, it will remain in a pending state until a vote occurs in the next scheduled CCB meeting.

Voting Process

Discussion should not occur during the voting section of the CCB meeting. Identified participants for each stakeholder will be individually asked for a yes or no vote on the change request in question. The individual and their vote will be recorded.

If the vote on a change request receives a unanimous yes vote, the change request will be approved. If the vote on a change request receives a unanimous no vote, the change request will be rejected. If the vote on a change request does not receive a unanimous vote, the change request will be placed into a hold state. The change request will then reenter the discussion section of the next CCB meeting. The change request will be placed to vote for a second time at the CCB meeting succeeding the CCB meeting at which the change request reenters the discussion phase.

If the second vote on a change request receives a unanimous yes vote, the change request will be approved. Otherwise, it will be rejected. A maximum of two votes will exist for each change request.

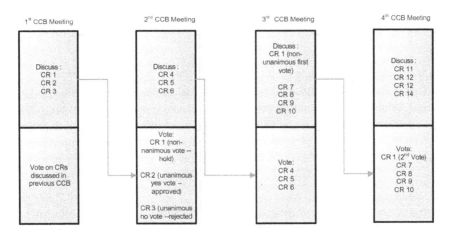

Figure 12. CCB Process

Project Plan/Timeline/Schedule

In 1916, Henri Fayol first described management in his classic description of management. He said "To manage is to forecast and plan, to organize, to command, to coordinate and to control."

Today's project management is not far from Fayol's reality. Based on Project Management Institute (PMI), there are five phases in managing a project. They are initiating, planning, executing, monitoring and controlling, and closing. One of the essential tools in project management to keep track of these phases is the project timeline, or the project plan.

Almost all project managers know how to set up a project plan. They know what the standard milestones or events for the project need to be. They plan the project accordingly. They plan the schedule according to a specific critical path, which are generally tasks. The traditional belief is that, once a project has missed a milestone, the project's staff cannot make up the time. Project managers may face the choice between extending the schedule and dropping the functions. The management part of project management is required to manage the schedule and include the functions. Here, we will discuss an alternative way of thinking.

As a project manager, if you can split the functions and give yourself sufficient flexibility in learning about the functions and project scheduling, then you can redirect the critical path and still make the schedule with the planned functions. This method of developing a number of small independent functions and frequent re-planning is iterative project management.

Multiple critical paths are in a given project. The task list generates a particular critical path. The people working on the project create another critical path. And hard resource availability creates yet another critical path. The true project critical path is the critical path through all three views: tasks, people, and resources.

During the initial planning phase of many projects, the tasks and events are planned. Hopefully, the task critical path emerges. Many project managers are also aware that people and resources, that is, machines, networks, and so forth, have an impact on the critical path. They plan to use these scarce resources appropriately.

In a project where the project manager and technical staff do not have sufficient knowledge of the full function set under development, a traditional approach does not guarantee success. The traditional approach assumes the project manager knows and understands the critical paths of tasks, people, and resources. In a less fully specified project, it is unlikely that the project manager will know all the critical paths. The project manager will probably be surprised by new tasks that arise, unforeseen tasks, or new expertise may have to be developed. New resources may be required.

When project knowledge is imperfect, an iterative approach is the answer. Consider the following. Plan the major milestones. Estimate the function freeze. Determine the criteria by which the project staff can agree that these milestones have occurred. Plan each segment of the project as it crystallizes. Stay at least four weeks ahead of the current state. As each iteration completes, the project manager and technical staff have a better understanding of the project and the eventual product, so more complete planning can take place. By the time the project has reached the function freeze milestone, the tasks required to get to code freeze are well understood. By the time code freeze is reached, the rest of schedule can be laid out and planned.

This iterative approach reduces uncertainty for the current project work and allows replanning of the critical path at a number of points in the project.

Milestones are key to success of this process. Each iteration can be a large milestone. Smaller milestones should be defined within that iteration. Project management and the team must agree on milestones and understand the critical nature of meeting them. In the iterative process, the project manager plans the milestones at a high level in each iteration and iterates on the work on a daily bases between the milestones. This process is more like handing out homework each day based on what has been discovered the previous day.

Even for an iteratively planned project, some tasks are clearly defined in each phase. For example, when a user acceptance test (UAT) is planned, then all the tasks and iterations prior to the tests need to be completed before the test can start. These tasks and iterations can and should be planned in the initial project schedule. Any tasks that can be planned in advance should be planned. Usually, these tasks are at a higher level, that is, iteration level.

One of the benefits of not doing detailed planning of the next major phase is that the project can advance more quickly. Some people are intimidated and get confused with large plans. They either think they cannot possibly make any progress or they figure it is not a big deal if their task slips because there are so many tasks.

However, any task slippage diminishes the ability to replan the rest of the project. If the project manager shows people a project plan with less detail and continually asks them for more detail, they are more motivated to complete their tasks. In my experience, people are anxious to complete their work and get the next batch of work. When there is huge task list of everything that needs to be done, people get bogged down.

By planning the current iteration in detail and gradually increasing the detail on the next iteration, people can see how progress is being made. They come up with possibilities to accelerate the project that the project manager may have missed.

In a fixed date schedule, the project manager is always looking for ways to complete the project early. But, in a traditional planning process, completing tasks early is generally wasted because:

- There is no rush to start the next task, so the task owner starts at the last minute.

- When people multitask between different tasks, they waste time changing context between tasks.

- Dependencies between steps can waste all advances, if the dependencies between steps and resources are not uncovered and planned before the tasks are started.

In an iteratively planned project, no one person has a huge list of tasks, so lack of progress is more visible. Because there are fewer tasks, there is incentive to start each task as quickly as possible so that forward progress can be reported.

A fixed date project has a deep sense of urgency, so the project manager can reduce the requests for and effects of multiple project multitasking. Using an iterative planning approach, the schedule becomes increasingly detailed over time. The dependencies are uncovered early. Replanning can occur when more dependencies are uncovered. Replanning becomes necessary when tasks do not complete on time or tasks complete ahead of schedule. Time cannot be made up. Only plans can change.

In an iterative project, you have choices beside slipping the schedule or limiting scope. For example, if you understand the current critical path by task and person performing that task, there may be an alternative to who performs the task at what time. This will enable the project manager to alter the critical path. If the critical path cannot be shifted, then the project manager only has the two choices: reducing scope or slipping the schedule.

The basis for iterative planning is keeping the focus on iteration and milestones within them instead of the traditional process of focusing on tasks. This process also sets the expectation for replanning efforts. Almost all projects replan at some point. This process will set the expectations for replanning. The work can then be accounted for. Critical path in this process becomes a tool to set priorities and inform management of the realities of the project. In the iterative process, two timelines are in the project:

- **Discovery Phase Timeline:** You will collect all needed information for the project. You will concentrate on the process of creating the business models and defining iterations by groups of functions as well as building and unit testing within each iteration. You will also create templates for all your baseline documents. The project charter and implementation timeline will be created during this phase. This phase would have a project timeline all on its own, but it is a short one. However, it is separate from your implementation timeline.

- **Implementation Phase Timeline:** One of your primary deliverables from the discovery phase, this is the main timeline that you will use to manage your project.

Creation of Implementation Timeline

A project timeline must be manageable. Project timelines with thousands of entries requires an army of planners to manage. You will spend a lot of time creating it just to watch it not resemble any reality at all after a few weeks. I cannot emphasize enough that the focus is on iterations and milestones, not how detailed the tasks are. In our iteration process, project timeline is a guide and map for the next steps. You do not have to capture every task at a detail level in the plan.

You can use several tools to create your plan, depending on the complexity of your project. No matter what tool you use, you should always start with a work breakdown structure (WBS), a results-oriented family tree that captures all the work of a project in an organized way.

It is often portrayed graphically as a hierarchical tree, but it can also be a tabular list of element categories and tasks or the indented task list that appears in your Gantt chart schedule. In our iterative process, we define the WBS elements by functions that application should perform. Starting a WBS is not an easy task. Most project managers and planners have a hard time with this process. One of your biggest allies in this process is the expertise of your team who has implemented your particular COTS application before. They should help you define the milestones and iterations. The second part is to focus on iteration as a whole and milestones within them rather than the activities.

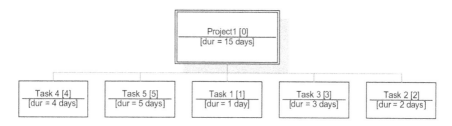

Figure 13. WBS example.

You do not want to complicate the plan more than it needs to be. If we assume the top level is the overall project (level 0), then the next level can start describing the actual iterations that the project will complete. After the iterations are described, the milestones can be defined that are required to build, test, and deliver each iteration. The timeline is ultimately comprised of activities, but they need to be developed in the context of completing iterations. The best option is to place the major iterations directly at level 1 and break the deliverables into smaller milestone components on the next level. The following outlines the steps needed to create your iterative plan:

- Collect all baseline documents. Review your project charter to ensure an understanding of what is to be produced, the overall time frame, risks, and assumptions, and who has what responsibility.

- Create your WBS. Start with the business model maps. Determine the groups of functionality that must be completed per iteration for the entire project to be completed. At this point, make sure that groups of functions are set up and you can identify the start and finish of each iteration. For instance, a traditional breakdown in an iteration might be planning/analysis/design/construct/test. You should also group by some work breakout, such as extract data/load data/report on information in all iterations that require that type of work. The initial high-level breakdown of work is called level 1. The point of the WBS is to capture all functions within the iteration.

- After you finish your initial breakdown of the work, do a quick estimate to determine if any of the pieces in an iteration require a work effort that is larger than the estimating threshold. The estimating threshold is usually eighty hours of effort. Depending on the size of your project, you can define it to be larger or smaller. If you have a medium to large project, most of the first level of work is still going to be larger than the estimating threshold. Look at these large pieces of work. Determine what activities are required to complete them. You can also break down work that is already less than the threshold. This gets you to level 2 of the WBS. When the process is complete, again estimate the work of the level 2 activities to see if they are still larger than the estimating threshold. If so, then they need to be broken down further. Your project plan should not go any deeper than level 3.

You have already done a high-level estimate of effort to determine if the work for each activity is greater than the estimating threshold. When the WBS is complete, you need to review and provide a specific estimate of effort for all of the detailed activities per iteration. The detailed activities are the ones at the lowest level that are not broken down any further.

Project Plan Synchronization Procedure

Large COTS implementations are composed of several different project plans. You usually have to coordinate efforts with several other systems that should be changed or enhanced as a result of your project. More than likely, these system enhancements have their own development process and methodology because they have been in place before your project. Each of these plans has dependencies with other plans. These interdependencies need to be synchronized to reflect the proper dates when predecessors are complete so successors may begin. To accomplish this, use touch points between plans that will be manually synchronized on a weekly basis so your project schedule will be accurate. The following procedure outlines the key steps and schedule that will be executed each week to ensure the schedule is accurate.

Plan Creation Requirements

When conditions within a project plan are recognized where deliverables, decisions, code, and so forth that are delivered in one plan are needed as inputs to another plan, a touch point will be defined in each plan that uniquely identifies the dependency. The planners will assign each touch point a unique number. The number will be typed into the appropriate user text field within the project plan. In the notes/memo area of the activity, each touch point will have a text description that defines its purpose. This description is critical to understanding the purpose of the touch point during future project work. The same description should be used in all plans. Each touch point activity should be assigned to resources who are responsible for delivering the needed information, that is, the push, as well as to resources who are assigned to validate accurate delivery of information, that is, the pull. Each touch point should be free-floating and not constrained in any way.

Plan Synchronization Process

On a scheduled basis, project planners will perform the following actions: update project plan with timesheet data; correct obvious errors, for example, typos; and run touch point schedule report for all touch points in the plan.

Planners from each team will also meet as a group and synchronize plans via the following rules. Synchronize based on comparing all pull touch points to the date of the push touch point. Set the date of all touch points to the date of the push. Synchronize all plan touch points. Once all plan touch points have been synchronized, compare the dates for critical path items.

If the scheduled date exceeds the original planned date by two weeks, that is, ten business days, or less, the planners log an issue in the issue management system stating the date issue, that is, the current project schedule is projecting ready for integration testing to be seven workdays late. It will be recommended that the team lead be assigned the task of resolving the issue. In most cases, it is expected that the area causing the issue will be assigned to resolve the issue.

If the scheduled date exceeds the original planned date by more than two weeks, that is, more than ten business days, the planners log an issue in the issue management system stating the date issue, that is, the current project schedule is projecting ready for integration testing to be seven workdays late. It will be recommended that the project leadership team member be assigned the task of resolving the issue. In most cases, it is expected that the area causing the issue will be assigned to resolve the issue.

The planner will write a short report and forward to the project leadership team, summarizing issues logged and noting any important trends or insights. The PMO will organize a formal meeting following these steps, which covers the project synchronization report as part of the standard meeting agenda. The PMO will take further action as appropriate.

Risk Management

In any project, there are risks. If they are managed and thought about in advance, the project team will be prepared to deal with them. In its role as the governance body of the project, the PMO has the responsibility of managing risks within the project.

What is risk management? There are several answers to this question, depending on who you ask. We will be discussing the aspects of risk and risk management within the confines of software development and COTS implementations.

According to Kloman, risk management is a discipline for living with the possibility that future events may cause adverse effects (Kloman 1995). In other words, based on calculated tasks and plans, we expect a certain number of adverse effects that a project team should be prepared to deal with. For a risk to be understandable, it must be expressed clearly. Such a statement must include a description of the current conditions that may lead to the loss and a description of the loss.

Projects using software risk management to manage their risks have realized benefits, including prevention of schedule delays, reduced project cost, more predictable schedules, and better attainment of customer commitments.

Based on Software Engineering Institute (SEI), philosophy risks are managed in two distinctive ways:

- **Continuous Risk Management:** When using continuous risk management, risks are assessed continuously and used for decision-making in all phases of a project. Risks are carried forward and dealt with until they are resolved or they turn into problems and are handled as such.

- **Noncontinuous Risk Management:** In some projects, risks are assessed only once during initial project planning. Major risks are identified and mitigated, but risks are never explicitly looked at again.

In an iterative environment, you should use the continuous process. This will enable you to keep a continuous track on potential risks and determine when mitigation plans should be executed. This process also enables project managers to close obsolete risks and open new ones as soon as the project identifies them.

At first glance, risk management might appear to just add complexity to an already complex undertaking. In reality, however, risk management activities make software projects less complex. Consider the following:

- Identification and prioritization of risks enables project managers and project staff to focus on the areas with the most impact to their project.

- Appropriate risk mitigation actions reduce overall project risk, which actually accelerates project completion.

- Projects that finish sooner cost less. Plus, risk mitigation actions can further reduce project cost.

- Projects using software risk management have more predictable schedules. They experience fewer surprises because they have identified and, in many cases, eliminated risks before they can become problems.

Risk management helps projects secure their customer commitments. Further, managers and project staff utilizing risk management have a better overall understanding of their project and make better decisions.

Implementation of Risk Management

Good risk management plans will includes the following aspects:

- Top-down risk estimation/Bottom-up risk management
- Identify and prioritize risks
- Carry out risk mitigation actions
- Monitor and adjust execution
- Conduct risk assessments

Top-down Risk Estimation/Bottom-up Risk Management

Top-down risk estimation maps project risk into schedule completion dates. This model enables project risk to be quantified in terms of a specific level of confidence (0 to 100 percent) or potential schedule slippage.

Bottom-up risk management puts detail behind the top-down approach. Bottom-up risk management identifies underlying project strengths and risks that drive the top-down risk estimate. The power of software risk management is realized by taking action to leverage project strengths and reduce and eliminate risks.

This activity provides a top-down perspective on project risk and determines an overall risk framework for a project. These models enable informed decisions about schedule commitments and contingency. Tools to develop a risk framework include top-down schedule metric, statistical project profile, and project schedule simulation.

- The top-down schedule metric uses project staff member knowledge, perspectives, and expectations to determine a project risk profile. As such, it can also reflect the impact of risk management action. As risk mitigation actions reduce project risk, the risk profile will shift up. At a given level of confidence, the projected completion date will shift left. These shifts reflect improved confidence in the project's ability to achieve customer schedule commitments.

- The statistical project profile looks at project size and software industry productivity models to develop a model of project risk. This model enables software organizations to evaluate factors that will make them more or less productive than the industry overall. Software organizations can then select a level of confidence that defines an achievable project completion commitment.

- A project schedule simulation can be accomplished using a tool such as Risk+ from Program Management Solutions, Inc. Based on probability distributions for individual tasks, the simulation will construct a statistical model of project risk. For simulation to provide useful results, the project schedule must be accurate and complete. Missing tasks, underscoped or overscoped tasks, and missed or invalid task or resource dependencies will result in garbage in-garbage out (GIGO) results.

Identifying and Prioritizing Risks

After the top-down perspective has been developed, the underlying reasons for the risk profile need to be determined. This is accomplished by identifying and prioritizing individual risks for the project. Individual risks can be identified using a variety of approaches based on reviewing published lists of project risk sources, including evaluating requirements specifications, project plans, WBS, Gantt or PERT schedules, and so forth; interviewing project staff; and brainstorming.

Risks can be prioritized through several methods. Some projects have used A-B-C or high-medium-low lists. Others have estimated the individual risk likelihood of occurring and the potential schedule impact to produce an overall rating for each risk. Experience shows that risks that impact critical path tasks should always have highest priority. Brainstorming for risk identification can often be completed more quickly and comprehensively with the help of a facilitator skilled in risk management practices. This strategy can also provide essential training for organizations and project staff who are unfamiliar with risk management practices.

Risk Mitigation Actions

Risk identification and prioritization activities are only useful if actions are defined and executed to mitigate risks. Aggressive, proactive risk mitigation actions for top-priority risks are essential to achieve the benefits of risk management. Risk mitigation actions are defined individually for project risks. In some cases, immediate action will be called for. In others, future consideration will be more appropriate.

For example, user interface requirements may be a risk on a particular project. To mitigate this risk, develop prototypes and use a iterative development process model. Another risk might be establishing host communication for the test environment. This risk could be reevaluated during later phases of development. At which point, a preliminary test environment can be constructed.

Monitoring and Adjusting Execution

Risk management is an integral part of project execution. As a project proceeds, some risks will be eliminated, but some new risks may also occur. Some risk mitigation actions will work well, but some may not work. New action will need to be taken. As the project proceeds, priorities will change. New risk management planning will need to be undertaken.

For example, a risk related to host communication may be eliminated, but end user system capacity may become a new risk for initial deployment. Prototypes may solidify user interfaces, but testing with unskilled operators may not work. An alternative strategy may be required. Setting up software development environments may be a high-priority risk early in a project, but testing environments will become much more important as the project proceeds. Monitoring project risks can be accomplished through the following mechanisms: scheduling risk mitigation tasks; reviewing milestones on the project schedule; holding formal project risk management review meetings; and conducting regular, anonymous surveys of project staff.

The project schedule is an excellent tool for risk management. By scheduling explicit risk mitigation tasks, progress and effectiveness can be reviewed on a timely basis at project status meetings. Further, schedule milestones can serve as a reminder of formal project risk management review meetings, which provide a forum for evaluation of project risks and the effectiveness of risk mitigation actions.

At project risk management review meetings, new risks can be identified. All project risks can be reprioritized, and new risk mitigation actions can be planned. This review should take a holistic approach to a project, considering all core and supporting areas for effective project execution. Regular, anonymous surveys provide a mechanism to gather feedback from all project staff, efficiently allowing them to provide input on current project risks. With large projects, this can be the only practical way to gather input from all staff. After consolidation, the survey results can be used as a basis for evaluating risk mitigation actions and planning new actions to address risks.

Summary

Risks are an inevitable part of COTS projects. Risk management is simply a practice of systematically selecting cost-effective approaches for minimizing the effect of threat realization to the organization. All risks can never be fully avoided or mitigated simply because of financial and practical limitations. Therefore, all organizations must accept some level of residual risks. Risk management is not an exact science. By reviewing the risk plan periodically, the PMO can adjust the probability and/or impact of these risks. They may rise to the top ten, and they can be brought to the attention of senior and project managers or other stakeholders who are in a position to either stimulate corrective actions or make a conscious business decision to proceed despite the risks.

Chapter Nine

Testing Concepts

Life Cycle Testing Concepts

Full life cycle testing is defined as the process of verifying the consistency, completeness, and correctness of software and related work products, such as documents and processes, at each stage of the development life cycle.

The purpose of a testing method is to provide a structured approach and discipline to testing. It includes test planning, managing and controlling the testing process, and testing techniques. The full life cycle testing methodology being introduced here outlines the generic testing processes and techniques needed to test applications. This methodology is targeted for the iterative project teams, that is, business and technical staff.

This chapter will take you through the concepts that are necessary to successfully test a software product under development. It outlines a full life cycle testing methodology.

A critical element in the successful development of any software application is effective testing. Testing moves the evolution of a product from a state of hypothetical usefulness to proven usefulness. It includes the testing of requirements, design, systems' code, documentation, and operational procedures. It is an inseparable part of the development of a product, which the purchaser and end user view as beneficial and meeting their needs. Testing is one of the ways in which a product achieves high quality. Iterative helps improve the quality of the product as well as the test process itself.

When testing responsibility falls outside of the scope of the development team, reference is made to external testing processes for completeness purposes only. As preparations are made to pass the system to a group outside of the development team for testing, it is expected that the project development team will consult the external group or their documentation for guidance.

The full life cycle testing methodology has three parts: testing concepts, test process model, and testing standards.

Testing concepts describes the why and what of the testing discipline. It presents the concepts relating to test planning, test preparation, test execution, and test reporting. It covers, at a generic level, every facet of testing, including types, techniques, levels, and integration approaches.

The test process model describes the how, who, and when of testing. It explains the processes, procedures, and tools needed to support a structured approach to testing.

Testing standards describe the criteria to be met in order for specific levels of testing, for example, operability testing, to be considered acceptable by the organization. In most organizations, the QA group owns and manages the standards.

Testing courses is a document that should teach the concepts of testing a software application by using the full life cycle testing approach. It will reinforce them with a case study that applies these processes, tools, and techniques.

Because this is a generic methodology, we will only be describing tools and techniques that are generic to testing. The descriptions will be at a level that will give you the concept of what the tool or technique is and its relevance to the testing process. Inspections are one example of such a technique. The reader may pursue additional education at a greater level of detail outside of this methodology.

It is suggested that anyone who is a novice to testing should read the concepts document completely and/or attend the course. Experienced test or development personnel can use this chapter as reference. It is expected that the testing process model content will be tailored to meet the unique needs of your application, project life cycle, and testing requirements. Testing standards, where available as part of organizational standards, will be used alongside the test process model to ensure the application development is conducted according to the needs of the organization.

Benefits and Costs of a Standardized Testing Process

The benefits of a standardized testing process include the following:

- Quality improvements will result from test involvement at the beginning of the life cycle.

- Better defined test cases will improve quality of the test effort and product.

- Opportunity to reuse test cases and have defined regression test cases will result in better test coverage.

- By involving designers of test plans and test cases, we ensure the product matches the design of the solution.

- By ensuring all test teams perform a postmortem or release review, the process will continue to be improved.

- It encourages reuse and sharing of resources and a consistent level of testing throughout the organization.

- It should allow for test resources to be correctly sized at the commitment phase of a project.

- Cost savings will be realized by finding problems earlier in the cycle. This applies particularly to finding problems before they go into production.

The costs involved include the following:

- Some projects may require additional reviews and tracking.

- Additional costs related to new tools, depending on what tools are used, may be required.

- Some educational costs, either for education on the test methodology or using specific tools, may be required.

- More work will be done in the initial test planning stages, but smoother execution of the later test phases should offset this.

Any additional costs of following the process should be minimal. The benefits, especially for medium to large projects, will outweigh them. The process has been designed so that there are fewer tasks for small projects than for larger projects. The effort should be commensurate with the result. Deployment of the process should definitely result in a better quality product, fewer defects post-production, and so forth.

Testing as Part of the Process

For implementing this new process, the full life cycle test methodology is being used. This method recognizes that the test team needs to be involved at every phase of the product/application through the concept phase as well as design, development, and deployment of each iteration. Test is not an afterthought. It is also not something that somebody else, who is unrelated to the development team, does. The testers for a given product should be an integral part of the team, as they perform a definite, valuable function. For those projects where there is substantial user testing, the development test team should be working with them to ensure their part of the test effort will have good coverage, tracking, problem reporting, and so forth.

Test planning begins for a project or program when requirements are accepted. Testing completes when the last phase of preproduction testing is complete, the application has been in production for a defined period of time, and all reviews are complete and documented, including test postmortems. The recommendation is to track problems for two weeks after a medium or large project has been moved to production.

Application Phases

1	Concept Phase	• A representative from the test team is sometimes involved in this phase to represent the end user.
2	Requirements Commitment Phase	• A test team must be involved in sizing test requirements, for example, hardware, software, personnel, and so forth. • No commitments to project/application should be made while there is uncertainty about the test resources needed. • Upon commitment, the overall project or program test lead must be identified.
3	Detailed Requirements/ Macro Design	• Once the first draft of the detailed requirements or macro design has been published, the test group starts planning a test strategy. • If used, a test strategy (scope) document is written • Someone from the test group approves all drafts of the specification and any design change documents or change requests. • Test cases are now outlined. Some may be fully written • The master test plan is started. It may be completed in this phase or next.
4	Code Phase	• This phase includes high-level design, low-level design, coding, and unit testing. • The master test plan is completed, published, and approved. • Test case creation continues. • Test cases for the initial formal test phase are completed and reviewed. • Test plans for the various test phases are started. • The one for the first formal test phase is completed, reviewed, and approved

5	Formal Test Phase	• The test plan for each phase is executed, and the results are tracked. • As one phase is being executed, the development of test cases for the next phase may still be ongoing. • The test plan for subsequent phases may be modified based on the results found during a test phase. • Entrance and exit reviews are held at the beginning and end of the phase, respectively.
6	Deployment Phase	• The test team must sign off if the product/application is ready to deploy • The test team needs to be aware of any problems arising in the first two weeks of deployment. This way, they can see if there was any way that these problems could have been found during one of the test cycles. • Postmortem/release/project reviews are held. The results are folded back into the test process.

Table 12. Various product/application phases.

Testing Fundamentals

Testing is conducted to ensure you develop a product that will prove to be useful to the end user. The primary objectives of testing assure that the system meets the users' needs (has the right system been built) and the user requirements are built as specified (has the system been built right.) The secondary objectives of testing are to:

• Instill confidence in the system through user involvement

• Ensure the system will work from both a functional and performance viewpoint

• Ensure the interfaces between systems work

• Establish exactly what the system does (and does not do) so the user does not receive any surprises at implementation time

• Identify problem areas where the system deliverables do not meet the agreed upon specifications

• Improve the development processes that cause errors

Achieving these objectives will ensure the associated risks of failing to successfully deliver an acceptable product are minimized, a high-quality product (as the application purchaser and user view it) is delivered, and the ability to deliver high-quality applications is improved. The purpose of a testing method is to provide a framework, set of disciplines, and approach for testing a software application so the process is consistent and repeatable.

Definition

Testing is the systematic search for defects in all project deliverables. It is the process of examining an output of a process under consideration, comparing the results against a set of predetermined expectations and dealing with variances. Testing will take on many forms. As the form and content of the output change, the approaches and techniques used to test them must be adapted. Throughout the discussion of testing concepts, we will use several terms that are fundamental:

- **Validation:** This is the act of ensuring compliance against an original requirement. An example is the comparison of the actual system response of an online transaction to what was originally expected, requested, and finally approved in the external design.

- **Verification:** This is the act of checking the current work product to ensure it performs as specified by its predecessor. The comparison of a module's code against its technical design specifications document is one example.

- **Process:** This is a series of actions performed to achieve a desired result that transforms a set of inputs, for example, information, into useful outputs.

- **Expectation:** This is a set of requirements or specifications to which an output result of a process must conform in order to be acceptable. One such example is the performance specification that an online application must return a response in less than two seconds.

- **Variances:** These are deviations of the output of a process from the expected outcome. These variances are often called defects.

Testing is then a process of verifying and/or validating an output against a set of expectations and observing the variances.

Ensuring Testability

Another important, but difficult, term to clarify is what is meant by a testable condition. To illustrate the definition, let's discuss "expectations" further. In order to be able to assess if an output meets or exceeds a given expectation, an expectation itself must be stated in testable terms. That is, when the characteristics of an output under test are compared against the expected characteristics, they can be matched in a clear and unambiguous way. You would not request that the answer to a calculation of one plus four to be an appropriate amount. To be testable, you would specify the answer as a single value like five or as a range between zero and ten if the exact answer were not known. If the result of the test were anything other than five or a number within the specified range, the test would unequivocally fail. You would record the variance. The example, of course, is trivial, but it serves to illustrate the point.

While you may strive to have requirements stated in testable terms, it may not always be possible. The required level of detail when you document and test the requirements might not yet be available. The process of requirements specification and external design should evolve the functional request from a collection of imprecise statements of user needs to testable user specifications. (See "Requirement Types" in chapter five.)

Even though the root of the word "specification" is specific, achieving specific requirements is an extremely challenging exercise. At every point in the specification process, you can check the testability of the requirement or specification by ensuring it is SMART. This acronym stands for Specific, Measurable, Attainable or Achievable, Realistic, and Timely. These specifications will form the basis for the criteria upon which the system purchaser and end user test and ultimately accept the system.

Testing Principles

The following are some powerful basic principles of testing. Although they are expressed simply and most of them appear to be intuitive, they are often overlooked or compromised.

- An author must not be the final tester of his or her own work product.
- While exhaustive testing is desirable, it is not always practical.
- Expected results should be documented for each test.
- Both valid and invalid conditions should be tested.
- Both expected and unexpected results should be validated.
- Test cases should be reused. That is, there are no throwaway test cases unless the work product itself is throwaway.
- Testing is a skilled discipline. It is on par with such skills as technical coding and analysis.

- Testing is a no-fault process of detecting variances or defects.

No-fault Testing

The introduction of variances is a normal and expected consequence of the human activity of developing any product. How many times have you heard, "To err is human"? This implies that testing should be a no-fault process of variance removal.

Testing is a cooperative exercise between the tester and developer to detect and repair defects that the development process has injected into the product. It should be apparent to anyone who has tested that this process of removing defects is complex and demanding, which only a skilled team of personnel can accomplish. They must use good techniques and tools in a planned and systematic way.

At the end of a development project, the team hopes that testing has been so successful that they do not have to invoke the last half of that famous saying, "To forgive is divine!"

Entrance and Exit Criteria

The concept of establishing prerequisites, that is, entrance criteria, and post-conditions, that is, exit criteria, for an activity to be undertaken is extremely useful for managing any process. Testing is no exception.

Entrance criteria are those factors that must be present, at a minimum, to be able to start an activity. In integration testing, for example, before a module can be integrated into a program, it must be compiled cleanly and have successfully completed unit testing. If the entrance criteria of the next iteration have been met, the next iteration may be started even though the current iteration is still underway. This is how overlapping schedules are allowed.

Exit criteria are those factors that must be present to declare an activity completed. To proclaim system testing completed, two criteria might be that all test cases must have been executed with a defined level of success (if other than 100 percent) and there must be no more than a mutually agreed upon number of outstanding problems left unresolved. Exit criteria must be specifically expressed using terms such as, "X will be accepted if Y and a Z are completed." For example, you may view the user acceptance test as the exit criteria for the development project.

Testing Approaches

Testing approaches fall into two broad classes: static and dynamic testing. Both are effective if applied properly. They can be used throughout the application life cycle. Testing tools and techniques will share characteristics from both these classes. The development and test teams are responsible for selecting and using the tools and techniques best suited for their project.

Static

Static testing is a detailed examination of a work product's characteristics to an expected set of attributes, experiences, and standards. Because the product under scrutiny is static and not exercised, for example, a module being executed, its behavior to changing inputs and environments cannot be assessed.

Discovering variances or defects early in a project will result in less expensive and less painful changes. In the development cycle, the only early testing usually available during preconstruction phases is static testing.

Some representative examples of static testing are plan reviews, requirements walkthroughs or sign-off reviews, design or code inspections, test plan inspections, and test case reviews.

The following is an example of how a static test would be applied in a walk-through of a single statement in a functional specification, "If withdrawal request is greater than $400, reject the request. Otherwise, allow subject to ATM cash dispensing rules and account balance."

The static test questions would include:

- Are all ATM dispensing rules the same on different types of machines?

- Do the ATM dispensing rules allow for withdrawals up to $400?

- Is the account balance always available? If not, what then?

- What multiples of amounts are allowed?

- What types of accounts are allowed?

- If the host is not available, do we use the card balance?

- If the host is unavailable but a deposit preceded the withdrawal request, should this be taken into account?

- If the request is denied, what is the message to the customer?

Seemingly complete and precise requirements can, with practice, generate many questions. If these questions are answered as soon as the specification is written, testing costs will be much less than if the questions are not asked until after coding has commenced. In the iterative process, we use static testing for documentation validation. (See "Document defect process.")

Dynamic Testing

Dynamic testing is a process of verification or validation by exercising or operating a work product under scrutiny and observing its behavior to changing inputs or environments. Where a module is statically tested by looking at its code documentation, it is executed dynamically to test the behavior of its logic and response to inputs. Dynamic testing used to be the mainstay of system testing and was traditionally known as testing the application.

Some representative examples of dynamic testing are application prototyping, executing test cases in an working system, simulating usage scenarios with real end users to test usability, and parallel testing in a production environment.

Testing Techniques

Three common testing techniques are black box testing, white box testing, and error guessing. The technique that looks at how a unit under test behaves by only examining its inputs and outputs is said to be a black box approach. Testing techniques that examine the internal workings and details of a work product are said to use a white box approach. These are explained more thoroughly later. The error guessing technique is where experience and intuition are applied to look for unexpected, but prevalent, errors.

Black Box Testing

In the black box approach, the testers have an outside view of the system. They are concerned with what is done, not how it is done. Black box testing is requirements and/or specifications-oriented. It is used at all test levels.

The system or work product is defined and viewed functionally. To test the system, all possible input combinations are entered. The outputs are examined. Both valid and invalid inputs are used to test the system. Examples of black box testing are entering an ATM withdrawal transaction and observing expected cash dispensed as well as exercising a program function with external data and observing the results.

White Box Testing

In the white box approach, the testers have an inside view of the system. They are concerned with how it is done, not what is done. White box testing is logic-oriented. The testers are concerned with the execution of all possible paths of control flow through the program.

The white box approach is essentially a unit test method, which is sometimes used in the integration test or operability test. Technical staff almost always performs it. Examples of white box testing are testing of branches and decisions in code and tracking of a logic path in a programmer.

Error Guessing

Based on past experience, test data can be created to anticipate those errors that will most often occur. Using experience and knowledge of the application, invalid data representing common mistakes a user might be expected to make can be entered to verify the system will handle these types of errors. An example of error guessing is hitting the Control key instead of the Enter key for a PC application and verifying the application responds properly.

Full Life Cycle Testing

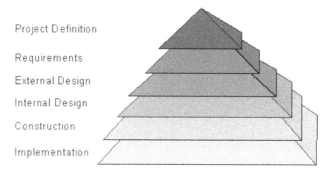

Figure 14. Application development iteration.

The software development process is a systematic method of evolving from a vague statement of a business problem to a detailed functional and concrete representation of a solution to that problem.

The development process itself is subdivided into a discrete number of iterations that align to a life cycle representing major stages or iteration of system evolution. At the termination of each phase, a checkpoint is taken to ensure the current phase is completed properly and the project team is prepared to start the next phase within that iteration. The process we use to define and build a software product is the application development life cycle. The testing process will align to these same phases. The development and test activities will be coordinated so they complement each other.

As the developer creates each interim work product, it is, in turn, tested to ensure that it meets the requirements and specifications for that phase so the resulting work products will be constructed on a sound foundation. This strategy of "testing as you go" will minimize the risk of delivering a solution that is prone to errors or does not meet the needs of the end user. We refer to testing at every phase in the development process as full life cycle testing. It will test each and every interim work product delivered as part of the development process.

Testing begins with requirements and continues throughout the life of the application. During application development, all aspects of the system are exercised to ensure the system is thoroughly tested before implementation. Static and dynamic, black box and white box, and error guessing testing approaches and techniques are used.

Even after an application has been in production, testing continues to play an important role in the systems maintenance process. While an application is being maintained, all changes to the application must be tested to ensure it continues to provide the business function it was originally designed for, without impacting the rest of the application or other systems with which it interfaces. When the hardware or software environment changes, the application must be retested in all areas to ensure it continues to function as expected. This is often referred to as regression testing.

What Is Tested

Those on a system development or maintenance team usually test the following:

- The function of the application system manual and automated procedures in their operating environment to ensure it operates as specified

- Exception (error) conditions that could occur to ensure they will be handled appropriately

- The interim deliverables of the development phases to demonstrate they are satisfactory and in compliance with the original requirements

The Testing Team

Developing a system requires the involvement of a team of individuals that bring varied resources, skills, experiences, and viewpoints to the process. Each plays a necessary role. Each may play one or more roles. The roles may change over the complete life cycle of development.

Added to the roles of sponsor, user, and developer defined in the application development process is the tester. The tester's role is to validate and verify the interim and final work products of the system using both user and operational product and technical expertise where necessary

In many cases, the sponsor and user are a single representative. In other cases, a special group of user representatives act as surrogate end users. While they may represent the end users, they themselves will usually never directly operate or use the application.

An organization where both the development team and user and/or sponsor personnel participate in the testing process is strongly recommended. It encourages user buy-in and acceptance through early involvement and participation throughout the development life cycle. Some benefits are:

- Involvement of developers and users in walkthroughs and inspections of the deliverables during the earlier phases of the development life cycle serves as a training ground for the developers to gain business knowledge.

- Testing will be more thorough and complete because users with greater product knowledge will be involved to test the business functions.

- The user acceptance testing will provide a formal validation of a more completely tested system rather than serve as a process where basic product defects are being uncovered for the first time.

- User personnel will become familiar with the forms and procedures to be used in the new system prior to implementation.

- Users who gain experience in using the system during the test period will be able to train other user personnel and sell the new system.

It is important to note the following.

- The extent of user participation will depend on the specific nature of your project or application.

- The user should only get involved in hands-on dynamic testing when the system is stable enough that meaningful testing can be carried out without repeated interruptions.

- Each user representative must be responsible for representing his or her specific organization and providing the product knowledge and experience to effectively exercise the test conditions necessary to sufficiently test the application.

- The test team is responsible for making certain that the system produced by the development team adequately performs according to the system specifications. It is the responsibility of the test group to accept or reject the system based on the criteria that were documented and approved in the test plan.

Traditionally, users are viewed as being from the business community. They should also be considered as being from the technical (computer) operations area. Systems should incorporate the requirements of all the groups that will use and/or operate the services provided by the system being developed.

Finally, while the technical staff may build the technical components of the application, they will also assume the role of tester when they verify the compliance to design specifications of their own work or work of others. This is an example of changing roles that was mentioned earlier.

The Testing Process

The basic testing process consists of four basic steps. They are plan for the tests, prepare for the tests, execute the tests, and report the results.

Testing is an iterative process. These steps are followed at the overall project level and repeated for each level of testing required in the development life cycle. This process is shown in the following test process overview diagram. The development of the application will be undertaken in stages. Each stage represents a known level of physical integration and quality. These stages of integration are known as testing levels. They will be discussed later.

The levels of testing used in the application development life cycle are unit testing, integration testing, system testing, system integration testing, user acceptance testing, and operability testing,

The master test plan is the first layer of plans and tests and addresses the overall project at a high level. Successive levels of testing will each be handled as additional refinements to the master test plan to meet the specific needs of that level of testing. The iterative methodology refers to these as detailed test plans. They are explained in more detail later.

For a more detailed treatment of the process, refer to the iterative models in the later sections of this chapter. The overview of the process is depicted as a level 0 data flow model. Each of the major processes on the level 0 data flow diagram has its own data flow diagram, which are shown separately on the following pages.

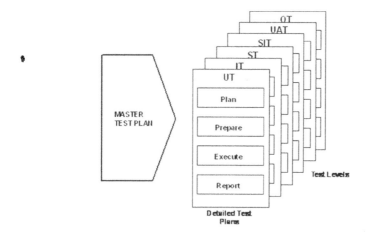

Figure 15. Testing steps.

Test Planning

Planning itself is a process. Performing each step of the planning process will ensure that the plan is built systematically and completely. Documenting these steps will ensure the plan is itself testable by others who must approve it. Most of the topics under planning should be familiar to all but the novice developer or tester. The test process model will lend some guidance in this area. A few topics deserve special attention because they are specific to testing or help in understanding testing in general.

The Administrative Plan

This portion of the plan deals with test team organization, test schedules, and resource requirements. These plans should be fully integrated into the overall project schedules.

We will more fully cover the specifics of test team planning later.

Risk Assessment

Why is risk assessment a part of planning? It gains an understanding of the potential sources and causes of failure and their associated costs. Measuring the risk prior to testing can help the process in two ways. High-risk iterations can be identified, and more extensive testing can be performed. Risk analysis can help draw attention to the critical components and/or focus areas for testing that are most important from the system or user standpoint. In general, the greater the potential cost of an error in a system, the greater the effort and the resources assigned to prevent these errors from occurring.

Risk is the product of the probability of occurrence of an error and the cost and consequence of failure. Three key areas of risk that have significant influence on a project are project size, experience with technology, and project structure.

The potential cost/risk factor, independent of any particular error, must considered when developing an overall testing strategy and a test plan for a particular system. (For more details, review chapter eight again.) One approach to assessing risk is:

- List what can go wrong during the operation of the application once implemented and the likelihood of occurrence.

- Determine the cost of failure. For example, consider loss of business, loss of image, loss of confidence in the system, security risk, and financial risk for each of these problems to the organization if it occurred.

- Determine what level of confidence is required and what critical success factors are from an application development and testing point of view.

- Develop a strategy and subsequent plans to manage these risks. This will form the basis of the testing strategy.

- Determine how much effort and expense should be put into testing.

- Determine when the potential loss exceeds the cost of testing. At that point, the testing is cost-justified

Test Focus

The overall objective of testing is to reduce the risks inherent in computer systems. The methodology must address and minimize those risks. Areas are identified to assist in drawing attention to the specific risks or issues where testing effort is focused and which the test strategy must handle.

So far, we have discussed the importance of quality of systems being developed and implemented. It is virtually impossible and economically not feasible to perform exhaustive testing. We must avoid both undertesting and overtesting while optimizing the testing resources and reducing cycle time. All of these lead to the question of management of conflicts and trade-offs. When projects do not have unlimited resources, we have to make the best use of what we have. This comes down to one question. What are the factors or risks that are most important to the user or client, developer from a system perspective, and service provider, which is usually computer services? The answer lies in considering the focus areas and selecting the ones that will address or minimize risks.

Test focus can be defined as those attributes of a system that must be tested in order to assure the business and technical requirements can be met. Some of the commonly used test focus areas are auditability, continuity of processing, correctness, maintainability, operability, performance, portability, reliability, security, and usability.

You may consider and include other focus areas as necessary. For example, technology may be a test focus in a cooperative processing environment. Compatibility of software may be a test focus item for vendor packages.

Each of the items on the list is a potential factor that may impact the proper functioning of the system. For example, the risk of the system not being usable may result in certain functions not being used. The challenge to effective testing is to identify and prioritize those risks that are important to minimize and focus testing in those areas. It is therefore critical that the users and developers make a joint decision as to what is important and what is not. It should not be decided from a single perspective.

To a major extent, correctness is most likely a high-priority test focus for most applications. Further considerations are:

- What degree of correctness is required?
- What are the risks if the functions are not tested exhaustively?
- What price are the users willing to pay?

That is, the process of determining test focus areas must be selective and selected focus areas must be ordered in terms of priority.

Essentially, the concept of risk and risk evaluation makes the decision of how much testing to do or what types of testing are needed to be performed as an economic decision. The economics of testing and risk management determines if defects are acceptable in the system. If so, what is the tolerable level of residual defects? That is, the decisions of what gets tested are thoroughly shifted from the judgment of the developers and users to ones based more objectively on economics.

Test Objectives

From a testing standpoint, the test objectives are a statement of the goals that must be achieved to assure the system objectives are met and the system will be demonstrated to be acceptable to the user. They should answer the questions, "What must be achieved? And when?" Test objectives must be able to assure that the system is at the level of quality that the acceptor of the system will expect and he or she will also be confident that the developer has achieved these expectations.

Test objectives should draw the attention or focus on the major testing tasks that must be accomplished to successfully complete full testing of the system. The purpose of developing test objectives is to define evaluation criteria to know when testing is completed. Test objectives also assist in gauging the effectiveness of the testing process.

Test objectives are based on business functions, technical requirements, and risks. Test objectives are defined with varying levels of detail at various levels of testing. There will be test objectives at the global cross-functional level as well as the major functional level. For example, if correctness of bank statement processing is to be a focus area, then one testing objective will concentrate on how correctness will be thoroughly proved in bank statement processing by the functional testing results.

Test Strategy

Test strategy is a high-level, system-wide expression of major activities that collectively achieve the overall desired result as expressed by the testing objectives.

For example, if performance (transaction response time) is a focus area, then a strategy might be to perform stress/volume Testing at the integration test level before the entire system is subjected to system testing. Similarly, if audit ability is a focus area, then a strategy might be to perform rigorous audit tests at all levels of testing.

As part of forming the strategy, the risks, constraints, and exposures present must be identified. These considerations must be accommodated in the strategy. This is where the planner can introduce significant added value to the plan.

One example of a strategy that handles constraints is if you have to develop the application to run on two technical platforms but only one is available in the development environment. The strategy might be to exhaustively test on one platform and test the other platform in the production operating environment as a parallel run. This strategy recognizes the constraint on the availability of test platforms and manages it with acceptable risk.

Another practical area of constraint may be where the organization's testing standards play a significant part in reducing the freedom you can adopt in your strategy.

All strategy statements are expressed in high-level terms of physical components and activities, resources, types and levels of testing, schedules, and activities. The strategic plan will be specific to the system being developed and will be capable of being further refined into tactical approaches and operating plans in the detailed test plans for each level of testing.

Strategic plans will drive future needs in resources or schedules in testing or development. They will often force trade-offs. Fortunately, because this is usually well in advance of the anticipated need, the project will have enough time to respond.

Detailed test plans should repeat the exercise of reviewing and setting objectives and be strategy-specific to each level of testing. These objectives and associated strategies, which are often called approaches at the lower levels, should dovetail with their predecessor higher-level master test plan set of objectives and strategies.

Build Strategy

A set of testing plans will include the high-level list of items for which testing is needed to be performed. These are the lists of business functions and structural functions that testing activities will cover. These can be derived from business models that the architecture team creates. (For more information, review chapter four.) You may consider that these are testing blueprints and use them in the way that architects use blueprints as plans to guide them in their design and construction processes. These architect's plans are not like resource and schedule plans. They serve very different purposes. They are more like a functional roadmap for building test cases. Both these types of plans will exist on a development project. Both will share dependencies.

The build strategy is the approach to how the physical system components will be built, assembled, and tested. Overall project requirements, such as user priorities, development schedules, earlier delivery of specific functions, resource constraints, or any factor where there is a need to consider building the system in small pieces, will drive it. Each build can be assembled and tested as a stand-alone unit, but there may be dependencies on previous builds.

Because it is desirable to test a component or assembly of components as soon as possible after being built, there must be close coordination between the development team (builders) and test team (testers). There must be a close collaboration on what components are built first, what testing facilities must be present, how the components will be assembled, and how they will be tested and released to the next level of integration. This process should be outlined in the iteration plans for each iteration. The following figure describes four different build examples:

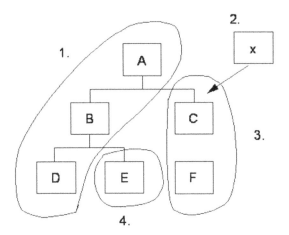

Figure 16. Sample build process.

Build 1 is an example of a well-defined functional build where each entity forms part of a single, clearly defined functional process. For example, an online selection of a single menu item will lead to several sequentially processed screens to complete the function. Development of all screen modules for this function would be grouped into one build.

Build 2 shows where a special test build is required solely to support testing. For example, in the illustration, entity X might be a driver program that needs to be developed to provide test data to entity C. Generally, these are throwaway entities. Test builds are especially critical to the overall project's schedule, and they must be identified as soon as possible. To illustrate this, if the need for the special program X is not identified until after coding of program C is completed, this will impact the testing schedule and, probably, the completion of program F.

Build 3 is a vertically sliced build where each entity is clearly sequenced in terms of its dependency. Usually, a vertical build is confined to discreet and relatively self-contained processes as opposed to functions. A good example of this would be in a batch process where an edit program would precede a reporting program. Each entity has its own functional characteristic, but it must clearly precede or succeed the other in terms of the development schedule.

Build 4 is a stand-alone build that is usually confined to a single, complex, or large function. A horizontally sliced build, which is not illustrated, is where similar, but independent, functions are grouped together. For example, programs B and C might be grouped together into one build, especially if the logic processes in each program are similar and can be tested together.

The diagram will also serve to illustrate the suitability of the different build types. Assume each box represents a program. B and C are updates; E and F produce simple batch reports. Also assume that no formal build design process was used. The update programs were logically assigned to one group and the report programs were assigned to another. These are, in effect, horizontally sliced builds. Probably the group working on the report programs would be finished first. Typically, this would be left to their own devices to create test data. When all programs are completed, they would be subjected to a system test that would discover errors in the reporting programs caused by inadequate testing, not bad coding. On the other hand, if a build strategy had been employed, the program assignment would probably use vertical builds where each update program and its supporting report program were built and tested in the same exercise, eliminating the need to create special test data for the report programs and reducing the likelihood of inadequate testing.

This is a simple example. On a complex project involving hundreds of programs and many development staff, a build strategy is critical. It will help to reduce testing time and may prevent the creation of unnecessary test data.

The business and structural function lists will be broken down into test conditions. Test conditions are grouped into test sets for purposes of test execution only. Test conditions may generate multiple test cases; test conditions can also be grouped into test cases. Individual test cases can be documented in preparation for execution. Test data is designed to support the test cases. The test case represents the lowest level of detail to which testing design is carried.

Even though the iterations are for the current project to use, some of the test sets from each of the iterations may be designated as part of the regression test set. When subsequent iterations are tested, the regression test sets may first be run before the actual test sets for the latest iteration. The collection of these test sets then becomes the regression test package. Similarly, the system test plan becomes the system documentation. The subsequent subset of test sets becomes the system test regression test package.

The test team will build test packages to test the system at the integration, system, and user acceptance levels of test. These test packages will consist of testing resource plans and test blueprint plans, cases, and data. The best way to create these packages is to start with unit test cases that were derived from each iteration's use cases. Each test package contains several functions and test cases for those functions. During integration and user acceptance testing, these functions will be aligned with business model lines and will be tested as a business process

For example, you are tasked with creating a Web site for a store. Based on your plan, you will build the Web site in two iterations: one for the back-end part that processes the order and one that creates the user pages and what the customers will see on the site. Your test team will create two test packages, one for each iteration during functional or unit testing. Each test package will only exercise one part of your application, either the front end or back end.

In order to ensure that your test process covers the entire business process, you test team will simulate a user connecting to the site and placing an order based on the business model that was created during the requirement phase. This process will utilize some of the test cases from each of the two development iterations. By utilizing this process test team, you will create a new test package for integration and user acceptance testing, a combination of the unit and functional test packages.

The level of detail included in the plans depends, of course, on the level of testing. An understanding of what will be tested will drive out other plans, such as test facilities requirements. The testing strategies will also influence these plans.

Chapter Ten

Problem Management and Change Control

Introduction

Problem management is the process by which problems, that is, variance reports, are controlled and tracked within a COTS project. This is a key tool to the testers. It is best to use the same problem management system that the overall project uses. If one does not exist, it should be set up early enough to be in place for the discovery of the first variances within all iterations. It is recommended that an automated system be used to capture, store, and report on the status of variances. Even on small projects, the amount of detail becomes enormous.

Change control or change management is similar to problem management in that it captures, stores, and reports on the status of valid and recognized change requirements. Change will impact testing teams. Again, an automated system should be used if the amount of change will be large. Once again, the project's change management system should be the one that everyone uses.

Plans should include provisioning for and using both problem management and change management systems. If these systems do not exist, plans should include provisions to create and maintain them.

Testing Methodologies

Test case design must focus on the testing techniques, tools, build and integration strategies, and basic characteristics of the system to be tested.

The first approaches to consider are black box and white box. Black box techniques help to validate that the business requirements are met; white box techniques facilitate testing the technical requirements. The former tests for requirements' coverage; the latter provides logic coverage.

The tools that provide the maximum payback are keystroke capture and play-back and test coverage tools. The underlying principles for both these tools are very simple. Keystroke capture tools eliminate the tedious and repetitive effort involved in keying in data. Several tools can be used in this process. For example, Rational and Test Director are applications that are commonly used for this process. Test coverage tools assist in ensuring that the myriad paths that the logic branches and decisions can take are tested. Both are very useful, but both need a lot of advance planning and organization of the test cases. As well as anticipating all expected results, testing tool procedures must provide for handling the unexpected situations. Therefore, they need a comprehensive test case design plan.

Care must be exercised in using these automated tools so as to get the most effective usage. If the use of these tools is not carefully planned, a testing team can become frustrated and discouraged with the tool itself. The testers will abandon these tools or fail to maintain the test cases already in their test packages.

The test design must also consider if the tests involve online or batch systems and if they are input- or output-driven. Test cases would be built to accommodate these system characteristics.

Another consideration is the grouping of valid and invalid test conditions. The integration approach, that is, top-down, bottom-up, or a combination of both, can sometimes influence the test case design.

Integration Approaches

A critical decision that impacts the implementation phase of the development process more than any other is the strategy to determine the sequence for developing and integrating system components, such as modules, programs, and subsystems. There are three strategies: top-down, bottom-up, or a combination of both. The project and test teams must make a conscious decision early in the development life cycle to merge the development and testing strategies so as to optimize the project resources and deliverables. Some opportunities to exploit advantages through integration approach when you consider system units that form a stand-alone subsystem and those that interface with other units, must exist before other units can be tested, or must be delivered first, which are critical to the success of the project, or those on the critical path of the project.

Top-down Approach

The top-down approach is a strategy that starts with construction of the top level or control modules. Then it integrates lower-level modules within the structure. In order to test the top-down approach, you will need to construct program and module stubs.

Stubs

A stub or dummy program simulates the existence of a program or module until the real module can replace it. This use of temporary code is an example of scaffolding. Each module integrated into the program or job stream requires stubs to represent the modules it calls until it is built. Testing can occur on the overall structure of modules itself and individual modules as part of the whole structure as they are integrated and come online.

Using stubs means there is a tendency to encourage the overlapping of design. Testing and incremental testing on a whole unit is performed at each integration. However, the stubs or dummies do require extra construction. Design deficiencies may not become apparent until lower-level modules are tested.

Bottom-up Approach

In the bottom-up approach, modules or program units are written and tested completely, starting at the lowest level. Successively higher levels are added and tested until the program or programs are complete.

Drivers

A driver is a program that simulates the calls to at least one modules under development to test those modules. For example, a driver may generate the data required for the module under test or read a file with test data, which is then formatted and passed to the module. Generally, a trace or debug report may be created, showing the data sent to and returned from the module. If the module being tested and any modules that it calls are fully coded, then the use of drivers is an effective approach to testing.

Development of driver modules or programs is sometimes thought to be a tedious process, which is often avoided. However, if such facilities are developed and fully documented, they can provide payback in the future for subsequent test exercises.

Drivers encourage reusable code, and they can be modified for other driver situations. However, they do require the construction of drivers, which means additional programming.

Top-down and Bottom-up Testing

The best features of top-down and bottom-up testing can sometimes be combined. Top-down testing is effective in iterative or incremental development strategies. Bottom-up testing is effective when several common modules are used by different systems and are normally coded and tested first. A combination of top-down and bottom-up strategies may be best depending on above considerations.

The development of regression test packages should be considered as part of the test design. Test cases should always be built for reuse. Test case design strategy entails the following steps:

- Examine the development/testing approach. This was explained in chapter one.
- Consider the type of processing, that is, online, batch, conversion program, and so forth.
- Determine the techniques to be used, that is, white box, black box, or error guessing.
- Develop the test conditions.
- Develop the test cases from use cases.
- Create the test script.
- Define the expected results.
- Develop the procedures and data, that is, prerequisites, steps, expectations, and post-test steps.

In developing a list of conditions that should be tested, it is useful to have a list of standard conditions to test for some common application types. A comprehensive list of considerations for ensuring a complete list of conditions to test is included later in this chapter. They can be used as an aid to develop test cases.

Levels and Types of Testing

Testing proceeds through various physical levels as described in the application's life cycle. Each completed level represents a milestone on the project plan. Each stage represents a known level of physical integration and quality. These stages of integration are known as testing levels. The levels of testing used in the application development life cycle are requirements testing, design testing, unit testing, integration testing, system testing, system integration testing, user acceptance testing, and operability testing.

In iterative methodology, requirements testing and design testing are used as additional levels of testing within each development iteration.

Testing Model

The descriptions of testing levels will follow. For each of these levels, these attributes will be covered: objectives, when to perform the tests, inputs/outputs, who performs the tests, methods, tools, and education/training prerequisites.

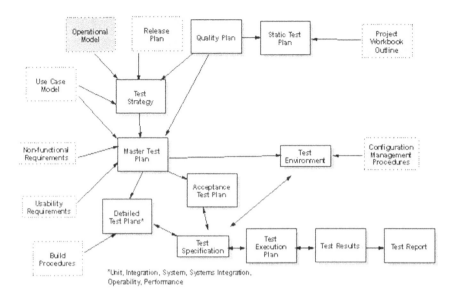

Figure 17. Testing Model

Requirements Testing

Requirements testing involves the verification and validation of requirements through static and dynamic tests. The validation testing of requirements will be covered under user acceptance testing. This section only covers the verification testing of requirements.

Objectives	• Verify the stated requirements meet the business needs of the end user before the external design is started • Evaluate the requirements for testability
When	• After requirements have been stated
Input	• Detailed requirements
Output	• Verified requirements
Who	• Users and developers
Methods	• Joint architectural document • Static testing techniques • Checklists • Mapping • Document reviews

Tools	• Document test process
Education	• Application training

Table 13. Requirements testing.

Design Testing

Design testing involves the verification and validation of the system design through static and dynamic tests. The validation testing of external design is done during user acceptance testing. Validation testing of internal design is covered during unit testing, integration testing, and system testing. This section only covers the verification testing of external and internal design.

Objectives	• Verify the system design meets the agreed upon business and technical requirements before the system construction begins • Identify missed requirements
When	• After external design is completed • After internal design is completed
Input	• External application design • Internal application design
Output	• Verified external design • Verified internal design
Who	• Users and developers
Methods	• JAD • Static testing techniques • Checklists • Prototyping • Mapping • Document reviews
Tools	• Document review process • Prototyping tools
Education	• Application training • Technical training

Table 14. Design testing.

Unit Testing

Unit testing is the initial testing of new and changed code in a module. It verifies the program specifications to the internal logic of the program or module and validates the logic.

Objectives	• Test the function of a program or unit of code such as a program or module • Test internal logic • Verify internal design • Test path an conditions coverage • Test exception conditions and error handling
When	• After modules are coded
Input	• Internal application design • Master test plan • Unit test plan
Output	• Unit test report
Who	• Developer
Methods	• White box testing techniques • Test coverage techniques
Tools	• Debug • Restructure • Code analyzers • Path/statement coverage tools • Test scripts
Education	• Testing methodology • Effective use of tools

Table 15. Unit testing.

You should walk through programs and modules before they are integrated and tested. The programmer should do this review first. Then there can be a more formal way through a structured walkthrough or code inspection. The steps to prepare for unit testing are:

• Determine the development integration and testing approach, top-down, bottom-up, or combination of both.

- Determine the testing techniques to be used (white box) and the particular subtechniques that apply best to the level of testing, such as statement coverage, decision coverage, path coverage, equivalence partitioning, boundary value analysis, and so forth.

- Develop the test sets of conditions. Depending on detail, this will be one or more levels.

  Check for the following:

- All variables are explicitly declared and initialized.

- The initialization is correct after every processing level. Work areas are cleared or reset properly.

- Array subscripts are integers and within the bounds of the array.

- Reference variables are correctly allocated.

- Unexpected error conditions are handled correctly.

- File attributes are correct.

- End of file conditions are handled correctly.

During program development, design the test cases at the same time as the code is designed based on use cases. The advantages of test conditions/cases are that they are designed more objectively, not influenced by coding style, and not overlooked.

Integration Testing

Integration testing verifies proper execution of application components. It does not require that the application under test interface with other applications. Communication between modules within the subsystem is tested in a controlled and isolated environment within the project. This process will ensure communication and functionality between iterations.

Objectives	• Technically verify proper interfacing between modules and within subsystems
When	• After unit testing of modules
Input	• Internal and external application design • Master test plan • Integration test plan
Output	• Integration test report

Who	• Developers
	• Test team
Methods	• White box
	• Black box
	• Problem management
	• Configuration management
Tools	• Debug
	• Restructure
	• Code analyzers
Education	• Testing methodology
	• Effective use of tools

Table 16. Integration testing.

System Testing

System testing verifies proper execution of the entire application components including interfaces to other applications. Both functional and structural types of tests are performed to verify that the system is functionally and operationally sound.

Objectives	• Verify the system components perform control functions
	• Perform intersystem test
	• Demonstrate the system performs both functionally and operationally as specified
	• Perform appropriate types of tests relating to transaction flow, installation, reliability, regression, and so forth
When	• After integration testing
Input	• Detailed requirements and external application design
	• Master test plan
	• System test plan
Output	• System test report
Who	• Test team and users
Methods	• Problem management
	• Configuration management

Tools	• Recommended set of tools
Education	• Testing methodology • Effective use of tools

Table 17. System testing.

Systems Integration Testing

Systems integration testing verifies the integration of all applications, including interfaces that are internal and external to the organization. Hardware, software and infrastructure components are in a production-like environment.

Objectives	• Test the coexistence of products and applications that are required to perform together in the production-like operational environment, that is, hardware, software, and network • Ensure the system functions together with all the components of its environment as a total system • Ensure the system releases can be deployed in the current environment
When	• After system testing • Often performed outside of project life cycle
Input	• Test strategy • Master test plan • Systems integration test plan
Output	• Systems integration test report
Who	• System testers
Methods	• White box • Black box • Problem management • Configuration management
Tools	• Recommended set of tools
Education	• Testing methodology • Effective use of tools

Table 18. Systems integration testing.

User Acceptance Testing

User acceptance testing verifies the system meets user requirements as specified. The user acceptance test simulates the user environment and emphasizes security, documentation, and regression tests. It will demonstrate that the system performs as expected to the sponsor and end user so they may accept the system.

Objectives	• Verify the system meets the user requirements
When	• After system testing
Input	• Business needs and detailed requirements • Master test plan • User acceptance test plan
Output	• User acceptance test report
Who	• Users and end users • Test team
Methods	• Black box • Problem management • Configuration management
Tools	• Compare • Keystroke capture and playback • Regression testing
Education	• Testing methodology • Effective use of tools • Product knowledge • Business release strategy

Table 19. User acceptance testing.

Operability Testing

Operability testing verifies that the application can operate in the production environment. Operability tests are performed after or concurrent with user acceptance tests.

Objectives	• Ensure the product can operate in the production environment • Ensure the product meets the acceptable level of service as per the SLA • Ensure the product operates as stated in the operations standards • Ensure the system can be recovered/restarted as per standards • Ensure the Job Control Language (JCL) is as per standard
When	• Concurrent with or after user acceptance testing is completed
Input	• User acceptance test plan • User sign-offs from user acceptance plan (if available) • Operability test plan • Operations standards (as appropriate)
Output	• Operability test report
Who	• Operations staff • Test team
Methods	• Problem management • Change management
Tools	• Performance monitoring tools
Education	• None

Table 20. Operability testing.

Types of Testing

Testing types are logical tests, which may be conducted in isolation or as combined exercises. They will be performed during the physical levels of testing as previously described.

Success of the testing process depends on selecting appropriate types of testing necessary to meet the test objectives; determining the stages or levels of testing when these types of testing would be most effectively used; developing test conditions to meet the test evaluation criteria; creating test scripts/test data required to test the conditions above; and managing fixes and retesting. It should be noted that a test type can appear in more than one test level. Types of testing are broadly classified as functional testing or structural testing.

Functional Testing

The purpose of functional testing is to ensure the user functional requirements and specifications are met. Test conditions are generated to evaluate the correctness of the application. The following are some of the categories: audit and controls testing, conversion testing, documentation and procedures testing, error handling testing, functions/requirements testing, interface/intersystem testing, installation testing, parallel testing, regression testing, transaction flow (path) testing, and usability testing.

Audit and Controls Testing

Audit and controls testing verifies the adequacy and effectiveness of controls and ensures the capability to prove the completeness of data processing results. Their validity would have been verified during design. Audit and controls testing would normally be carried out as part of system testing once the primary application functions have been stabilized.

The objectives for audit and controls testing are to ensure or verify that audit trail data is accurate and complete, transactions are authorized, and audit trail information is produced and maintained as needed.

Examples include using hash totals to ensure the accumulation of detailed records reconciles to the total records, inspecting manual control availability and operation to ensure audit effectiveness, and reviewing the audit trail from the full parallel run to ensure correctness.

Conversion Testing

Conversion testing verifies the compatibility of the converted program, data, and procedures with those from existing systems that are being converted or replaced. Most programs that are developed for conversion purposes are not totally new. They are often enhancements or replacements for old, deficient, or manual systems. The conversion may involve files, databases, screens, report formats, and so forth. Portions of conversion testing could start prior to unit testing. In fact, some of the conversion programs may even be used as drivers for unit testing or to create unit test data.

The objectives for conversion testing are to ensure or verify that new programs are compatible with old programs; the conversion procedures for documentation, operation, user interfaces, and so forth work; converted data files and format are compatible with the new system; new programs are compatible with the new databases; new functions meet requirements; unchanged functions continue to perform as before; structural functions perform as specified; and backout/recovery and/or parallel operation procedures work.

Examples include converting from one operating system to another, converting from host to distributed systems, and converting from IMS databases to DB2 tables.

User Documentation and Procedures Testing

User documentation and procedures testing ensures the interface between the system and the people works and is useable. Documentation testing is often done as part of procedure testing to verify the instruction guides are helpful and accurate. Both areas of testing are normally carried out late in the cycle as part of system testing or in the user acceptance test. It is normally a mistake to invest a lot of effort to develop and test the user documentation and procedures until the externals of the system have stabilized. Ideally, the persons who will use the documentation and procedures are the ones who should conduct these tests.

The objectives are to ensure or verify that user or operational procedures are documented, complete and correct, and easy to use. Additionally, a person's responsibilities should be properly assigned, understood, and coordinated. Finally, users and operations staff should be adequately trained.

Examples include providing operations staff with manuals and having them use this information to run the test application. The operations staff would have their actions observed in a real operations simulation. Another example includes providing data entry personnel with the kind of information they normally receive from customers and verifying the information is entered correctly as per manuals or procedures. Finally, real end user scenarios are simulated using the system with the documentation and procedures developed.

Error Handling Testing

Error handling is the system function for detecting and responding to exception conditions, such as erroneous input. The completeness of the error handling capability of an application system is often key to the usability of the system. It ensures that incorrect transactions will be properly processed and the system will terminate in a controlled and predictable way in case of a disastrous failure. It should be noted that error handling tests should be included in all levels of testing.

The objectives are to ensure or verify that the system can detect all reasonably expected errors, the system can adequately handle the error conditions and ensure continuity of processing, and proper controls are in place during the correction process. Error handling logic must deal with all possible conditions related to the arrival of erroneous input, such as initial detection and reporting of the error, storage of the erroneous input pending resolution, periodic flagging of the outstanding error until it is resolved, and processing of the correction to the error.

Examples of error handling testing includes seeding some common transactions with known errors into the system or simulating an environmental failure to see how the application recovers from a major error.

Function Testing

Function testing verifies that each business function operates as stated in the requirements and as specified in the external and internal design documents. This occurs at each stage of development. Function testing is usually completed in system testing. By the time the system is handed over to the user for user acceptance tests, the test group has already verified to the best of their ability that the system meets requirements.

The objectives are to ensure or verify that the system meets the user requirements, the system performs its functions consistently and accurately, and the application processes information in accordance with the organization's standards, policies, and procedures.

Examples include manually mapping each external design element back to a requirement to ensure they are all included in the design (static test) or simulating a variety of usage scenarios with test cases in an operational test system.

Installation Testing

Any application that will be installed and run in an environment remote from the development location requires installation testing. This is especially true of network systems that may be run in many locations. This is also the case with packages where changes were developed at the vendor's site. Installation testing is necessary if the installation is complex, critical, should be completed in a short window, or of high volume, such as in microcomputer installations. This type of testing should always be performed by those who will perform the installation process. Installation testing is done after exiting from system testing or in parallel with the user acceptance test.

The objectives are to ensure or verify that all required components are in the installation package, the installation procedure is user-friendly and easy to use, the installation documentation is complete and accurate, and the machine-readable data is in the correct and usable format.

Examples include verifying the contents of installation package with its checklist of enclosures or actually having a person outside of the development or test team install the application using just the installation documentation as guidance.

Interface/Intersystem Testing

Application systems often interface with other application systems. Most often, multiple applications are involved in a single project implementation. Interface or intersystem testing ensures the interconnections between applications function correctly. Interface testing is even more complex if the applications operate on different platforms or different locations or use different languages.

Interface testing is typically carried out during system testing when all the components are available and working. It is also acceptable for a certain amount of interface testing to be performed during user acceptance tests to verify that system-tested interfaces function properly in a production-like environment. Interface testing in a user acceptance test should always be the first practical tests in order to resolve incompatibility issues before the users commence their tests.

The objectives are to ensure or verify that proper parameters and data are correctly passed between the applications, the applications agree on the format and sequence of data being passed, proper timing and coordination of functions exists between the application systems and processing schedules reflect these, interface documentation for the various systems is complete and accurate, missing data files are properly handled, it is not possible for the same file to be processed twice or to be processed out of sequence, and implications are clearly identified if the interfacing applications are delayed, not available, or have been cancelled.

Examples include taking a set of test transactions from one application to be passed to another application and passing them into the interfacing application or simulating the loss of an upstream interface file in a full system test.

Parallel Testing

Parallel testing compares the results of processing the same data in both the old and new systems. Parallel testing is useful when a new application replaces an existing system, the same transaction input is used in both, and the output from both is reconcilable. It is also useful when switching from a manual to an automated system. Parallel testing is performed by using the same data to run both the new and old systems. The outputs are compared. When all the variances are explained and acceptable, the old system is discontinued.

In those situations where the old system was satisfactory, the objectives are to ensure or verify the new system gives results consistent with the old system.

However, in those circumstances where the old system was unsatisfactory, expected differences in results should occur.

One example includes running the old system, restoring the environment to what it was at the beginning of the first run, and then running the new version in a production environment. Another example includes executing two manual procedures side by side and observing the parallel results.

Regression Testing

Regression testing verifies that no unwanted changes were introduced to one part of the system as a result of making changes to another part of the system. To perform a regression test, the application must be run through the same test scenario at least twice. The first test is run when your application or a specific part of your application is responding correctly. Your application's responses to the first test serve as a base against which you can compare later responses. The second test is run after you make changes to the application. The application responses are compared for both executions of the same test cases. The results of comparison can be used to document and analyze the differences. By analyzing the differences between two executions of the same test cases, you can determine if your application's responses have changed unexpectedly.

The developer should always use regression testing during unit testing. In conjunction with a change management discipline, it will help prevent code changes from being lost or overwritten by subsequent changes. Once all the function is stabilized and further changes are not expected, a final regression test should be done as the final act of system testing.

The objectives are to ensure or verify the test unit or system continues to function correctly after changes have been made and later changes do not impact previous system functions.

Examples include running a final test of a group of changes by executing a regression test run as the last system test or reusing accumulated test cases during follow-up unit tests on a module each time an incremental change is coded.

Transaction Flow Testing

Transaction flow testing can be defined as the testing of the path of a transaction from the time it enters the system until it is completely processed and exits a suite of applications. For example, if it is an online branch transaction for issue of a draft on another bank, path testing starts when the branch teller enters the transaction at the terminal. It then goes through account debiting, draft issuance, the funds transfer to the paying bank, draft settlement, account reconciliation, and reporting of the transaction on the customer's statement. This implies that transaction flow is not necessarily limited to testing one application especially if more than one system application handles the end-to-end process. Wherever any one component in a flow of processes changes, it is the responsibility of the person or group making that change to ensure that all other processes continue to function properly.

Transaction flow testing may begin once system testing has progressed to the point that the application is demonstrably stable and capable of processing transactions from start to finish.

The objectives are to ensure or verify the transaction is correctly processed from the time of its entry into the system until the time it is expected to exit; all the output from the various systems or subsystems, which are input to the other systems or subsystems, are processed correctly and passed through; interfaces can handle unexpected situations without causing any uncontrolled abends or break in services; and the business system functions seamlessly across a set of application systems.

Examples include entering an online transaction and tracing its progress completely through the applications or creating unexpected problem situations in interface systems and verifying the system is equipped to handle them.

Usability Testing

The purpose of usability testing is to ensure the final product is usable in a practical, day-to-day fashion. Whereas functional testing looks for accuracy of the product, this type of test looks for simplicity and user-friendliness of the product. It would normally be performed as part of functional testing during system and user acceptance test.

The objectives are to ensure the system is easy to operate from an end user and a service provider standpoint; screens and output are clear, concise, and easy to use; help screens or clerical instructions are readable, accurately describe the process, and are expressed in simple jargon-free language; and input processes, whether via terminal or paper, follow natural and intuitive steps.

Examples include testing a data input screen to ensure that data is requested in the order the client would normally use it or asking someone unconnected with the project to complete a balancing process on a printed report by following the instructions.

Structural Testing

The purpose of structural testing is to ensure the technical and housekeeping functions of the system work. It is designed to verify the system is structurally sound and can perform the intended tasks. Its objective is also to ensure the technology has been used properly. When the component parts are integrated, they should perform as a cohesive unit. The tests are not intended to verify the functional correctness of the system. Rather, they show the system is technically sound.

The categories covered in the next subsections are backup and recovery testing, contingency testing, job stream testing, operational testing, performance testing, security testing, and stress/volume testing.

Backup and Recovery Testing

Recovery is the ability of an application to be restarted after failure. The process usually involves backing up to a point in the processing cycle where the integrity of the system is assured and then reprocessing the transactions past the original point of failure. The nature of the application, the volume of transactions, the internal design of the application to handle a restart process, the skill level of the people involved in the recovery procedures, documentation, and tools provided all impact the recovery process.

Backup and recovery testing should be performed as part of the system tests and verified during operability testing whenever continuity of processing is a critical requirement for the application. Risk of failure and potential loss due to the inability of an application to recover will dictate the extent of testing required.

The objectives are to ensure or verify the system can continue to operate after a failure, all necessary data to restore/restart the system is saved, backed-up data is accessible and can be restored, backup and recovery procedures are well-documented and available, and people responsible for conducting the recovery are adequately trained.

Examples include simulating a full production environment with production data volumes or simulating a system failure or verifying that procedures are adequate to handle the recovery process.

Contingency Testing

Operational situations may occur that result in major outages or disasters. Some applications are so crucial that special precautions need to be taken to minimize the effects of these situations and speed the recovery process. This is called contingency.

Usually, users rate each application in terms of its importance to the company. Contingency plans are drawn up accordingly. In some cases, where an application is of no major significance, a contingency plan may be to simply wait for the disaster to go away. In other cases, more extreme measures must be taken. For example, a backup processor in a different site may be an essential element that the contingency plan requires. Contingency testing will have to verify that an application and its databases, networks, and operating processes can all be migrated smoothly to the other site.

Contingency testing is a specialized exercise that operations staff normally conducts. There is no mandated phase in which this type of test is to be performed. Although, in the case of highly important applications, this will occur after system testing and probably concurrent with the user acceptance tests and operability testing.

The objectives are to ensure or verify the system can be restored according to prescribed requirements; all data is recoverable and restartable under the prescribed contingency conditions; all processes, instructions, and procedures function correctly in the contingency conditions; and the system and all its processes and data can be restored when normal conditions return.

Examples include simulating a collapse of the application with no controlled backups and test its recovery and the impact in terms of data and service loss or testing the operational instructions to ensure they are not site-specific.

Job Stream Testing

Job stream testing is usually done as a part of operational testing. That is, it is performed during the test type, not the test level. But it is still performed during operability testing. Job stream testing starts early and continues throughout all levels of testing. Conformance to standards is checked in user acceptance and operability testing.

The objectives are to ensure or verify the JCL is defect-free, compliant to standards, and will execute correctly; each program can handle expected parameter input; the programs are generating the required return codes; jobs are sequenced and released properly; file formats are consistent across programs to ensure the programs can talk to each other; and the system is compatible with the operational environment.

Examples include having an operations staff member inspect the JCL, having a took like JCL Check inspect the JCL, running a full operating test with a final version of the operations JCL, or attempting to run the application with an invalid set of parameters.

Operational Testing

All products delivered into production must obviously perform according to user requirements. However, a product's performance is not limited solely to its functional characteristics. Its operational characteristics are just as important since users expect and demand a guaranteed level of service from computer services. Even though operability testing is the final point where a system's operational behavior is tested, it is still the responsibility of the developers to consider and test operational factors during the construction phase. Operational testing should be performed as part of integration and system Testing and verified during operability testing.

The objectives are to ensure that all modules and programs are available and operational; all online commands and procedures function properly; all JCL conforms to standards and operates the application successfully; all scheduling information is correct; all operational documentation correctly represents the application, is clear, concise and complete; and all batch functions can be completed within an acceptable window of operation.

Examples include simulating a full batch cycle and operating the process exactly as prescribed in the run documentation or subjecting all JCL to a standard check.

Performance Testing

Performance testing is designed to test if the system meets the desired level of performance in a production environment. Performance considerations may relate to response times, turnaround times (throughput), technical design issues, and so forth. Performance testing can be conducted using a production system, a simulated environment, or a prototype.

Attention to performance issues, for example, response time or availability, begins during the design phase. At that time, the performance criteria should be established. Performance models may be constructed at that time if the nature of the project warrants it. Actual performance measurement should begin as soon as working programs, but not necessarily defect-free programs, are ready.

The objectives are to ensure or verify the system performs as requested, for example, transaction response, availability, and so forth.

Examples include using performance monitoring tools to verify system performance specifications, logging transaction response times in a system test, or using performance-monitoring software to ensure identification of dead code in programs, efficient processing of transactions, and so forth. Normal and peak periods should be identified. Testing should be carried out to cover both.

Security Testing

Security of an application system is required to ensure the protection of confidential information in a system and verify other impacted systems are protected against loss, corruption, or misuse by either deliberate or accidental actions. The amount of testing needed depends on the risk assessment of the consequences of a breach in security. Tests should focus on and be limited to those security features developed as part of the system, but they may include security functions previously implemented but necessary to fully test the system. Security testing can begin at any time during system testing and continue in user acceptance testing. It is completed in operability testing.

The objectives are to ensure or verify the security features cannot be bypassed, altered, or broken; security risks are properly identified and accepted; contingency plans are tested; and the security that the system provides functions correctly.

Examples including attempting a sign-on to the system without authorization if one is required, verifying passwords are not visible on terminals or printed output, attempting to give yourself authorization to perform restricted tasks, or attempting to enter unauthorized online transactions to ensure the system can identify and prevent such unauthorized access as well as report it if required.

Stress/Volume Testing

Stress testing is defined as the processing of a large number of transactions through the system in a defined period of time. It measures the performance characteristics of the system under peak load conditions. Stress factors may apply to different aspects of the system, such as input transactions, report lines, internal tables, communications, computer processing capacity, throughput, disk space, input, output, and so forth.

Stress testing should not begin until the system functions are fully tested and stable. The need for stress testing must be identified in the design phase. It should commence as soon as operationally stable system units are available. However, it is not necessary to have all functions fully tested in order to start stress testing. It is started early so any design defects can be rectified before the system exits the construction phase.

The objectives are to ensure or verify the production system can process large volumes of transactions within the expected time frame, the system architecture and construction is capable of processing large volumes of data, the hardware/software is adequate to process the volumes, the system has adequate resources to handle expected turnaround time, and the report processing support functions, for example, print services, can handle the system's volume of data output.

Examples include testing system overflow conditions by entering more volume than the tables can handle, transaction queues, internal storage facilities, and so forth; testing communication lines during peak processing simulations; or using test data generators and multiple terminals, stressing the online systems for an extended period of time and stressing the batch system with more than one batch of transactions.

Relationship between Levels and Types of Testing

The following table illustrates the relationship between testing levels and testing types. The table shows the level(s) where each type of test might be performed. These are only suggestions. Obviously, each project has different characteristics, which have to be considered when planning the testing process.

As an example, attention is drawn to interface/intersystem testing. This is clearly a systems test function, but, given environmental constraints within the development facility, some interface testing may have to be performed as an initial process within user acceptance testing.

Levels	Unit	Integration	System	Systems Integration	User Acceptance Test	Operability
Types						
Audit and Control		■	■	■		
Conversion	■		■	■		■
Documentation and Procedure			■	■	■	■
Error Handling	■	■	■	■	■	■
Function/ Requirement	■	■	■	■	■	
Installation			■			■
Interface/ Intersystem			■	■	■	■
Parallel			■		■	■
Regression	■	■	■	■	■	■

Levels	Unit	Integration	System	Systems Integration	User Acceptance Test	Operability
Transaction Flow			■	■	■	
Usability			■		■	
Backup and Recovery	■		■	■		■
Contingency				■		■
Job Stream		■	■	■	■	■
Operational			■	■		■
Performance			■	■		■
Security	■		■	■		■
Stress/Volume			■	■		

Table 21. Relationship between Testing Levels and Types

Test Management

Data Setup

Setting up test data is a very tedious and time-consuming process. After the test case design has been selected, we have to consider all the available sources of data and build new or modify existing test data. Frequently, the testers tend to look at the functional specifications and set up data to test the specifications. This tends to overlook how the software will be used. It is therefore important that the production data is analyzed to understand the types, frequency, and characteristics of data so they can be simulated during testing.

While setting up test data, select from the following sources: production data, data from previous testing, data from centralized test beds (if available), and data used in other systems (for interface testing).

In many situations, data from the selected source(s) must be supplemented to cover additional conditions and cases. When setting up effective test data, the goal is to provide adequate requirements and conditions coverage. Try to include some of each of the following types:

- Frequently occurring types and characteristics of data that have high risk, for example, deposit or withdrawal transactions at a banking terminal
- Frequently occurring types of data with very little exposure, for example, maintenance-type transactions such as name and address changes
- Low-frequency errors that have very little consequence
- Low-frequency errors resulting in heavy losses, for example, the printing of a few additional zeros in a financial report

Once the data source has been identified, you must determine the files and file sizes to use. Always try to use any known standards or conventions for databases and files. Data are then extracted using the appropriate methods.

The key to successful testing is to state the expected results when defining the test conditions and documenting the test scripts. Documentation should include what is being tested, how testing is done (procedures), where to find the test data, and the expected results. The keys to reducing the effort to create test data are reuse and recycle!

Test Setup: Data and Procedure

The test procedures describe the step-by-step process to conduct the tests. The primary goal is to define the sequence and contents of tests and establish pass-fail criteria for each. In so doing, you will also be establishing the entry and exit criteria for each test.

As part of the process of setting up entrance criteria, we are defining the prerequisites and corequisites. For example, if we want to test the printing of certain audit reports in batch, we may include the entry of online transactions and the bringing down of the online system as entry criteria. Again, if we are testing for a specific error condition to be generated and reported on the audit report as part of our test, we may specify a particular entry appearing on the report to be the exit criteria. We cannot exit until that entry appears as expected.

Typically, test procedures include instructions to set up the test facility. For example, if files must be restored before a test is run, this becomes the first step in the test procedure. If certain tests fail, backout steps may have to be performed to undo what was done up to that point. In that case, some restart and recovery steps may be required once the problem has been fixed. All of these steps are included as part of the test procedure.

Sometimes, it might not be possible to anticipate all error conditions. In that case, steps to handle an unexpected error situation should be described.

Setting up procedures may also involve writing the JCL, or platform-specific equivalent, to be used in production. This is usually tested during system testing and certified in the user acceptance and operability test environment. If the JCL is being set up for a new job, it will actually be tested during integration and system testing before being promoted to user acceptance testing. Follow all relevant JCL standards for setting up the production JCL procedures.

Managing and Controlling the Test Effort

Although testing is a part of the development process, the activities that the test manager and staff must manage can be quite distinct and critical to the overall success of the project. The following are the major factors that are most important to testing. While some are exclusive to testing, others are shared as part of overall project management.

Project Plans and Schedules

In larger projects, the test manager will assume responsibility for the portion of the project plans that relate specifically to testing activities. It is important for the test team to institute a tracking and control system to measure the schedule's progress and identify potential bottlenecks. As an example, test plans are written to schedule and control test runs. These can be as complex and extensive as those that the product developers use. This activity can demand a level of planning skill on par with a project manager.

It is critical that the testing plans, including schedule, costs, and resources, be fully integrated with the development plans and be managed as an overall plan for all sizes of projects. This ensures that coordination is achieved throughout the project.

Test Team Composition and User Involvement

A key step in managing a successful test project is to identify the key participants who will be involved in testing. It is good to use the concept of a test manager. Typically, the test manager will be from the development team, but he or she can come from someone in the users' shop with experience in this or related areas. The role of the test manager is to customize the generic testing methodology; define test responsibility/tasks that need to be performed; identify individuals who can perform those responsibilities/tasks; and plan, coordinate, manage, and report results of the testing process.

The test team staff is responsible for producing test package material, including test cases, test data, and test procedures, and executing test cases, reporting results, and retesting fixes. The technical staff is responsible for providing the technical guidance required to test and fix the new application.

Personnel involved in testing activities can be typically drawn from any of the following groups: developers, users, user management, operations, or independent test group specialists.

Effective managing and control of the test effort requires that a test team leader and staff be assigned and the roles and responsibilities defined. For each level of testing, clearly communicate and document the following:

- Who creates the test data

- Who runs the tests or enters the data

- Who checks the results

- Who makes the decisions on what corrections are to be made

- Who makes the required corrections

- Who builds and maintains the test facilities

- Who operates the testing facilities and procedures, for example, output handling

Skills/Education

An important part of quality testing is the use of trained testers. This includes training on the application under test as well as general test techniques and methodologies. As test experience grows, so will the quality level of testing. As experience with an application grows, so will the amount of testing that can be accomplished in the same amount of time. Thus, it is vital to have support for retaining trained test personnel. The proposal document covers these areas of tester skills and education:

1	Management must recognize testing as a critical discipline	<ul><li>Effort must be made to retain experienced testers.</li><li>Testers must see a growth or career path in testing.</li><li>New testers should be assigned an experienced tester as a mentor</li><li>Reviews should reflect the test aspect of the job, as opposed to using one standard form for both testers and developers in an organization.</li><li>Effort must be made to encourage tester education.</li><li>Funding for courses directly related to test methodology and/or techniques should be included in yearly budgets.</li></ul>

2	Tester education has many aspects.	• Education must be provided for general testing and test methodology. • Education must be provided for testing of a specific item or piece of the solution. • Education must be provided on the test process. • Education must be provided in the business process supported by the application. • Education must be provided to develop the end user point of view. • Education must be provided for problem management tools • Education must be provided for test tracking tools. • Education must be provided for test automation tools.
3	Training in test methodology is critical.	• Training must be provided for test planning. • Training must be provided for test coverage of test cases and their variations. • Training must be provided for risk assessment/acceptance. • Indication for completion must be provided.

Table 22. Areas of tester skill and education.

Action	Large Project	Medium Project	Small Project
Educate all testers in the test process	Required	Required	Required
Educate testers in general test methodology	Required	Required	Recommended
Educate testers on project's problem management tool	Required	Recommended	Recommended
Educate testers on project's test case tracking tool	Required	Recommended	Recommended

Action	Large Project	Medium Project	Small Project
Educate testers in the details of the project's test cases	Required	Required	Required
Promote use of the test community Web site	Recommended	Recommended	Optional

Table 23. Skills education actions based on project size.

Measurement and Accountability

You cannot manage what you cannot measure. The test manager will track the typical project measures such as schedules and resources. Project teams are all accustomed to those. There should also be an objective set of measurements to track and control the progress of the testing activities and their success. Many of these measurements are just plain common sense. Many major project experiences have validated them. They can be applied at each level of testing. Among the parameters the test team must know are:

Coverage	• What parts have I completed testing successfully? • What parts have I attempted to test?
Defect Prediction	• How many variances can I expect?
Problem Management	• How many variances have I already discovered? • How many variances have I fixed and have left to fix? • What is the impact (seriousness) of the outstanding variances? • At what rate is the team still finding variances?

Table 24. Testing parameters.

While the list of questions may not be exhaustive, it does represent the most useful information the test team needs to know. Using the measures that answer the above questions and history of previous projects, the test planner can make more reliable schedule, resource, and test plans. Then he or she can use the ongoing results to control and report on the success of testing. The accountability of the team will rest on the outcome of these measures, but the risk will be managed over the full project life cycle.

At this point, the specific measures will not be discussed. The methodology training will refer to some of the more popular measures recommended. The measures that your project selects will depend on your needs.

Reporting

Progress reporting to management must be regular and useful. The format and frequency of the reports are the responsibility of the test manager or, in the absence of that position, the project manager.

To be useful, progress should be reported in terms of factual and objective measures. The measures, which answer the questions posed in the previous section, could be presented or combined and used to answer other related management questions. Graphic representation of the data improves the clarity and impact of the information. The level of detail should be appropriate to the audience to which you are reporting.

The test team should contribute to and be recipients of testing progress reports. Success of testing then becomes a visible incentive.

Problem Management

Once a work product is transferred from its author and becomes part of the test process, it becomes subject to problem management procedures. Any problem reported will be documented, tracked, and reported until it becomes resolved. There is a tendency not to report very small problems. This must be resisted because the impacts of the problem or its fix might not be fully analyzed. The problem may lose visibility for retesting and subsequent analysis.

The status of problems discovered and outstanding must be tracked and reported regularly. Using backlog measures, that is, where outstanding problems are accumulated, counted, and reported, you can assess the ability of the project team to cope with the volume and/or severity of problems. If the backlog continues to increase in relation to the numbers of problems discovered, then this information can assist in determining the need to change the project and test schedule. Similarly, if severe problems remain unresolved for prolonged periods, this might indicate design issues, which may need addressing.

Another benefit of maintaining a history of problems is the capability of the organization to improve the testing or development processes through causal analysis. For every problem, cause category codes can be assigned and later analyzed for patterns of failures on which to base corrective actions.

Causal analysis is a process whereby every problem's cause is tracked and categorized. Very often, a situation may cause multiple problems that manifest themselves in different forms and different places in a system. If these causes are not tracked, significant time can be wasted throughout a testing exercise. If they are recorded and categorized, identification of common problem-causing situations is facilitated.

If the project has a problem management system, it should be used. Otherwise, one should be created and maintained whether supported with automated tools or not.

Primary Business Roles

The primary roles are the defect submitter, QA lead, defect owner, and component lead. This process begins when a defect is entered against a documented system. All projects must use some form of problem tracking and reporting. As the size and formality of the project increases, so does the formality of problem tracking. For all test phases, you must determine who will manage problem tracking, what problem management process will be used, what tools will be used, and how status and measurements will be reported. The following provides a definition of the problem management process:

1. Cross organization/site implications (communication) are considered.

2. All interfaces must have agreement with severity criteria and process.

3. The recommended standard severity criteria includes the following:

   - Response Turnaround Time (RAT), a negotiable, good-faith effort based on severity level
   - Workaround Turnaround Time (WAT)
   - Solution (final fix) Turnaround Time (TAT)

The following table describes the defect severity and the suggested turnaround time, which can be customized for a particular project.

Area/ Project	Severity 1	Severity 2	Severity 3	Severity 4
Definition	• A general function does not work or creates incorrect output, creating a critical impact with no alternative available. • All tests or a major collection of tests are stopped.	• A general function does not work or produces incorrect output, creating a critical impact with an alternative or bypass available. • A particular function does not work or produces incorrect output with no alternatives available. • Test cases are capable to continue on most functions.	• A particular function does not work or produces incorrect output, but the problem is not critical. • There is a workaround; you are able to continue work on other test cases.	• There is degraded or limited use of a function, but circumvention is possible with no operational impact. • It is negotiable on specific problem.
WAT	24 hours	48 hours	4 days	4 days
RAT	N/A	N/A	11 days	14 days
TAT	48 hours	4 days	N/A	N/A

Table 25. Defect severity definition.

All problems found must be documented on a timely basis. Severity 1 and 2 defects must be reported the day they are found. Lesser severity problems should be reported by the end of the next business day. Problems found should be related back to the test case(s) that exposed them. Problems found should be related back to the component of the application where they were found. A procedure for verifying fixes should be in place. A procedure for handling defective fixes must be in place, that is, sending a defect back for rework because the fix does not fix the reported defect or does not fix the entire reported defect. Testers, developers, and all parties involved in test must be educated in the process and problem workflow.

1. Identify focal points for problem management from a test standpoint and reporting/measurement standpoint.

2. Realize that controlling the test environment is an integral part of problem/ environment management.

    *   Implement procedures for controlling the test environment.

    *   Identify procedures and schedules for installing fixes.

    *   Identify procedures for backing out fixes.

3. Define reports/measurements and the process for them.

    *   Define who will be receiving the reports and measurements.

    *   Determine how often the reports will be run.

Suggested report items include: number of problems open; number of problems closed; problems by severity; problems by resolver/business area; problems by root cause area (user interface, database, other component, and so forth); overdue problems; length of time to resolve problems by severity; rate of problems being opened; rate of problems being closed; number of problems by project/ release; number of problems found by a test case or group of test cases (problems by requirements); and tool(s) used.

All locations on the same project or program should use the common tools. Tool education must be provided for all involved parties, including testers, developers, and so forth. Education should be provided in the use of the tool, that is, mechanics. Education should be provided in how the selected tool supports the overall problem management process, that is, process flow.

Activity Diagram

The following diagram shows the flow of this process:

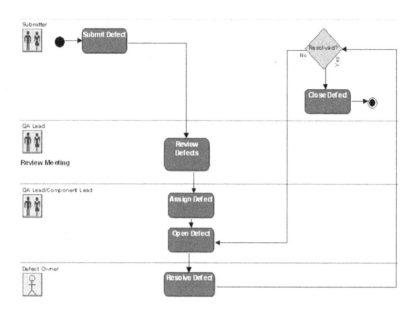

Figure 18. Activity flow.

Submit Defect

This activity represents the defect submitter creating a defect record in the defect system. Typically, document defects will be submitted by those assigned to review a component prior to a QAD meeting. QA will submit defects against the system.

Review Defects

This activity represents the review of defects during periodic reviews. For documents, the QA lead will review defects with the defect submitters at the QAD meetings. The purpose of the meetings is to review all newly submitted document defects that are in the submitted state at the appointed QAD time. The QA lead will lead the discussion on the defect's validity, severity, and owner. Weekly QAD meetings will be held to review cumulative defects entered for the weekly period.

For system defects, the QA lead will conduct daily triage meetings to discuss newly submitted system defects during test cycles within each iteration and during integration and user acceptance testing. The QA lead will discuss validity, severity, and other issues.

Valid or Invalid Defect?

If the defect is deemed as invalid, the QA lead must mark the defect rejected and move the defect to closed status. If the defect is deemed valid, the process flows to the next activity. Only the person who opens the defect can close the defect. During the test meeting, a consensus must be reached between the development group and person responsible for opening the defect. Your defect management system should not allow anyone except the person who opens the defect to close a defect.

Assign Defect

This activity represents the assigning of a defect within a defect management system. Specifically, the state of the defect should be moved from submitted to assigned. The QA lead will assign ownership of system defects while the component lead will assign ownership of document defects.

Resolve Defect

This activity represents the defect owner's responsibility to resolve any defects in the open state. The defect owner should place the defect in the resolved state upon resolution.

Resolved or Unresolved Defect?

This decision belongs to the original defect submitter. Once the defect owner has resolved the defect, the defect submitter is responsible for verifying the resolution. If the submitter agrees the defect is resolved, the submitter must proceed to close the defect. Otherwise, the submitter must follow up with the defect owner to further discuss the defect resolution. If the submitter is not satisfied with the defect resolution, the submitter must reject the defect. It will be escalated.

Escalation of defects will begin with the defect manager, who will monitor and attempt to resolved defects that are rejected. After a cycle of review and unsuccessful resolution, the defect manager will attempt to resolve the defect with the submitter and owner. If that attempt fails, the defect manager will escalate the defect to issue management system for senior and project management groups to resolve.

Close Defect

This activity represents the defect submitter's responsibility to close defects that are marked resolved after verifying the resolution. You should establish turnaround time for this activity to minimize the impact on schedule for meeting the exit criteria.

Action	Large Project	Medium Project	Small Project
Problem tracking tool used	Required	Required	Required
Reports presented to management at least weekly	Required	Required	Required
Problem analysis performed at end of a test phase or end of project	Required	Required	Required
Test environment strictly controlled	Required	Required	Required
Problem management tool education provided	Required	Required	Required

Table 26. Problem management actions based on the size of the project.

Change Management

When the system requirements or specifications are approved at each iteration level, they become candidates for change control. As part of the evaluation process for a change, the test team should be involved since the change may have a significant effect on the direction and cost of testing. It may also affect the test build strategy.

Failure to strictly adhere to formal change management has been the reason for the failure of many projects. Inadequate change control leads to runaway requirements, elongated test schedules, and inflated project costs.

If the project has a change management system, it should be used. Otherwise, one should be created and maintained whether supported with automated tools or not.

Configuration Management

As development progresses, the interim work products, for example, design, modules, documentation, and test packages, go through levels of integration and quality. Testing is the process of removing the defects of components under development at one testing level and then promoting the new defect-free work product to the next test level.

It is absolutely critical that the highest level of test not be corrupted with incomplete or defective work products. It might require the retest of some or all of the work products at that level to regain the state of confidence in their quality.

A test team member generally acts as the gatekeeper to the next level of test and assures the quality of the interim work products before they are promoted. Update access is restricted from the authors. Procedures and/or automation, such as software library control systems, may enforce control.

These controls are key to avoiding rework or defective work slipping by uncontrolled. A configuration or version control process and tools must be present and proactively managed throughout the project. Good PMO process will ensure integrity of the test system and documents. We have previously explained processes for configuration management control on documents and code promotion processes for system.

Reuse

This testing methodology assumes a process of creating an initial work product and then refining it to subsequent levels of detail as you progress through the stages of development. A master test plan is first created with a minimal level of detail known at the time. It is used as the template and source of basic information for the detailed test plans. The test sets, cases, and data are created and successively refined as they are used through the design, code/unit test, and integration test for use in the system test and user acceptance test. Even then, they are not discarded. They are recycled as the system test and/or user acceptance regression test packages.

The deliverables that the test team produces at one phase should be considered as candidates to be reused fully or, in part, by subsequent phases. The final product of all the testing should be the regression test package, which is delivered as part of the implementation to those who will maintain the system.

Other Continuous Improvement Actions

Continuous improvement is the goal of every organization. One of the key techniques for continually improving the test process is the postmortem or release review. Other methods are the causal analysis of problems found during test, analysis of problems that escaped test and went into production, and continuing test methodology education. The following are the continuous improvement actions from the test process.

Postmortem Review

A technique that most test groups are currently using is the postmortem or iteration review. Some groups have a general review that involves the team in the same meeting(s) as the test team. Other test groups will have a meeting on their own and discuss problems found and suggestions for improvement. These suggestions may be processes entirely within the scope of the test team, or they may be items involving code. After this, any problems or suggestions involving another team will be brought forward to that team. Suggestions of a general project nature are brought to the attention of the project manager.

Postmortem review(s) are required for large and medium projects. They are recommended for small projects. These usually take the form of a meeting involving the testers, project test lead, and test phase lead(s). The developers of the code are sometimes included. For programs, the program test lead may also participate or chair a postmortem at the program level. The output of the test postmortem is input to an overall postmortem or review of the project and/or program

Intermediate postmortem reviews must be held at the end of each formal test phase for large projects. This is recommended for medium projects, and it is optional for small projects. Postmortem review(s) should include what went right, what went wrong, and why. Root cause analysis should be done on severity 1 and 2 problems, and the code development team may be needed for this.

An analysis of errors that should have been caught earlier is done. "Earlier" may be in a previous test phase, including unit test, or possibly in a review of the solution design/specification.

Failed and blocked test execution record analysis is also completed. A metrics analysis is done, which reviews schedule changes and associated justifications, final defect count, defect arrival rate, and summary of measurement reports.

The team will also look at test plan items not tested and gather implementation feedback on lessons learned as well as suggestions and recommendations for process improvements.

Action items will be identified. The responsible person will be assigned. Due dates will be set. Someone must be assigned to track these items through to completion.

Items outside the scope of test that impact the program or project should be turned over to problem management. Suggested changes to the test process should be forwarded to a member of the cross-organizational test process team.

The test postmortem report template should be used. It should be stored in a central location for easy access by project managers and test team leads for all projects.

During testing, a postmortem log should be maintained. This would be a list of the issues to be brought forward at the postmortem review, and it should contain sufficient details to analyze the issue.

Other Postmortem Actions

Besides the results of postmortems and release reviews, other actions will aid in continuous improvement of test processes. Improvements may be to local processes, or they may be fed back to the cross-organizational team for updates to the process.

Analysis of problems reported after the application/product is in production mode may show problems that the test group could have caught during a formal test phase. If problems are found, either during test or in production, that show ambiguities or omissions in the detailed requirements and/or functional specifications, the test group can work more closely with the design/group on the review of test cases.

Analysis of the problems reported during a formal test phase may show a weakness in one particular area of the application. This information can then be fed back to development. The test area may want to put some extra emphasis on this area in the next test phase. This area may also warrant some extended regression testing in the next release.

Experiences with test tools should get fed back to the cross-organizational test team so they can start building a base of experiences to use when making recommendations. Good and bad experiences with the test process should be fed back to the cross-organizational test team so the process can be updated. The process is dynamic. It is not cast in stone.

Organizations should think about how to capture good ideas or suggestions for next time from the team. This could be a team room, document, file, and so forth. The form does not matter as long as there is a place for ideas to be held and not lost.

Regression test cases should be identified after each test phase or cycle in preparation for the next one. Any needed updates should be scheduled.

The use of orthogonal defect classification (ODC) on problem reports should be considered. While there is a learning curve on this, the groups that have used it for a while are seeing beneficial results. The following table describes the continuous improvement actions based on project size:

Action	Large Project	Medium Project	Small Project
Project/Program postmortem/review held and documented	Required	Required	Recommended
Review held after each formal test phase	Required	Recommended	Optional
Analysis performed on problems found in production	Required	Recommended	Optional
Suggestions for test process improvements feedback	Recommended	Recommended	Recommended
Regression test cases identified for next release	Required	Recommended	Optional
ODC used on defect/fault reports	Recommended	Recommended	Optional

Table 27. Continuous improvement actions based on project size.

In closing, I would like to emphasize the importance of testing in the overall project and COTS implementation process. In COTS and other projects, the emphasis should be on quality as well as on time and budget delivery of the project. Quality, measurable test process is key to accomplishing these tasks.

Closing Thoughts

Our approach's philosophy emphasizes the business-technical nature of organizational systems. It stresses the relationship between business and technical domains is one of co-evolution. This suggests it may be appropriate to consider these organizations as self-producing. They are not static. They are continually trying to reinvent themselves to exploit the opportunities that their dynamic environment present.

The decision to build or buy a large-scale information system is becoming increasingly important. Historically, organizations built customized, large-scale systems, but the trend over the last decade has reversed overwhelmingly toward the purchase of COTS based systems.

Too many organizations take an all-or-nothing view with regard to the use of COTS components in mission-critical systems. That is, either COTS components are never safe to use, or COTS use should be maximized. Factors that influence this decision include attributes of the COTS products themselves as well as attributes of the system's mission, the vendor, the vendor's development life cycle process, and your own organization's risk management skills.

The process in this book provides the architectural building blocks for developing flexible information systems that exploit their dynamic environment and incorporating COTS systems. Indeed, the use of COTS as components is a vital way of incorporating innovation into ongoing system development. The independent development of COTS is an opportunity as well as a problem. Innovation may arise through examining new COTS features, which cannot be predicted. One feature of this approach is that COTS systems are not considered special. Using dynamically located off the net services, open source software, and exploratory tools that users create are all examples of the exploiting emergent behavior of the dynamic environment. These require flexible integration mechanisms.

This framework can be used to develop flexible systems, where the emphasis is on run-time flexibility in the incorporation of COTS systems as components. By themselves, these systems can be the software development environments for other software systems. The same approach applies to the incorporation of COTS both at run time and during the development process. This framework does not incorporate a particular tool set for development process. It can integrate any set of COTS software development tools. Of particular interest is the case where both the developing software system and developed software system are architecturally sound and can live harmoniously within the current architecture.

There is considerable flexibility over the relationship between business and technical process. This process approach gives considerable flexibility in the integration strategy for the COTS components. Value chains of systems can be assembled.

A well thought-out and well-executed software project that incorporates one or many COTS solutions can happen more quickly and be more cost-effective than the same system implemented with custom-developed components. Too often, COTS projects are not thought out or planned, running on the incorrect assumption that every COTS solution is a small integration project without the issues and complexities discussed here. This way of thinking leads to unrealistic and poorly managed expectations, resulting in failed projects. These types of failures occur when project managers fail to plan for or incorporate the additional activities unique to COTS-intensive developments. Following this methodology will ensure that important activities and decision points are properly executed, reducing many of the risks associated with such developments.

References

Conferences and Papers

Albert, C., and L. Brownsword. 2002. Evolutionary Process for Integrating COTS-Based Systems (EPIC). In *SEI Technical Report CMU/SEI-2002-TR-005*, by the Software Engineering Institute at Carnegie Mellon University.

Avgeriou, P., N. Guelfi, and G. Perrouin. 2004. Evolution through Architectural Reconciliation. In *Electronic Notes in Theoretical Computer Science*, by the 2004 Software Evolution Through Transformations (SETra) workshop in Rome, Italy.

Bosch, J. 1999. Superimposition: A Component Adaptation Technique. *Information and Software Technology* 41: 257–73.

___. 2000. Design and Use of Software Architectures. Addison-Wesley.

Clements, P., R. Kazman, and M. Clein. 2002. Evaluating Software Architecture. Addison-Wesley.

Clements, P., F. Bachmann, L. Bass, D. Garlan, J. Ivers, R. Little, R. Nord, and J. Stafford. 2002. Documenting Software Architectures: Views and Beyond. Addison-Wesley.

Ganesha Web site

Garlan, D., R. Allen, and J. Ockerbloom. 1995. Architectural Mismatch: or Why It's Hard to Build Systems Out of Existing Parts. In *Proceedings of the International Conference on Software Engineering* at Seattle.

Grunbacher, P., A. Egyed, and N. Medvidovic. Reconciling Software Requirements and Architectures with Intermediate Models. *Journal of Software and Systems Modeling*.

Guelfi, N., B. Ries, and P. Sterges, P. 2003. MEDAL: A CASE Tool Extension for Model-driven Software Engineering. In *SwSTE '03 IEEE International Conference on Software—Science, Technology & Engineering in Hertzeliyah, Israel*.

Guo, G.Y., J.M. Atlee, and R. Kazman. 1999. A Software Architecture Reconstruction Method. In *WICSA-1 in San Antonio, Texas*.

Heineman, G. 1998. A model for designing adaptable software components. In *Twenty-second International Conference on Computer Software and Applications Conference (COMPSAC) in Vienna, Austria*, 121–127.

Hofmeister, C., R. Nord, and D. Soni. 1999. Applied Software Architecture. Addison-Wesley.

IEEE. 2000. Recommended Practice for Architectural Description of Software-Intensive Systems, *IEEE std. 1471–2000*.

Keller, R. and U. Hölze. 1997. Binary component adaptation. In *Technical Report TRCS97-20*, by University of California, Santa Barbara.

Kiczales, G., J. Lamping, C. Lopes, C. Maeda, A. Mendhekar, and G. Murphy. 1997. Open implementation design guidelines. In *Proceedings of the 19th international conference on Software engineering in Boston, Massachusetts, May 17–23*, 481–490.

Kruchten, P. 1995. The 4+1 view model of architecture. *IEEE Software*.

Medvidovic, N., and R.N. Taylor. 2000. A classification and comparison framework for software architecture description languages. *IEEE Transactions on Software Engineering* 1, vol. 26, 70–93.

Medvidovic, N., A. Egyed, and P. Gruenbacher. 2003. Stemming Architectural Erosion by Coupling Architectural Discovery and Recovery. In *Proceedings of the Second International Requirements to Architecture Workshop (STRAW 03) in Portland, Oregon, May 3–11*.

Mikic-Rakic, M., N.R. Mehta, and N. Medvidovic. 2002. Architectural Style Requirements for Self-Healing Systems. In *1st Workshop on Self-Healing Systems in Charleston*.

Perry, D.E., and A.L. Wolf. 1992. Foundations for the Study of Software Architectures. *Software Engineering Notes*.

The Portable Bookshelf. www.swag.uwaterloo.ca/pbs/.

SHriMP. http://shrimp.cs.uvic.ca/.

Szyperski, C. 1999. Component Software—Beyond Object-Oriented Programming. ACM Press.

Tran, J., and R. Holt. 1999. Forward and Reverse Architecture Repair. In *Proceedings of CASCON '99 in Toronto*, 15–24.

Tran, J., M. Godfrey, E. Lee, and R. Holt. 2000. Architecture repair of open source software. In *Proceedings of 2000 International Workshop on Program Comprehension (IWPC-00) in Limerick, Ireland.*

Tzerpos, V., and R.C. Holt. 1996. A Hybrid Process for Recovering Software Architecture. In *CASCON '96 in Toronto.*

Tu, Q., and M. Godfrey. 2002. An Integrated Approach for Studying Software Architectural Evolution, In *Proceedings of 2002 International Workshop on Program Comprehension (IWPC-02) in Paris, France.*

Welch, I., and R. Stroud. 1998. Adaptation of connectors in software architectures. In *Third International Workshop on Component-Oriented Programming in Brussels, Belgium.*

Publications

Abowd, G., et al. 1994. SAAM: A Method for Analyzing the Properties of Software Architecture. In *Proceedings of the 16th International Conference on Software Engineering in Sorrento, Italy, May 16–21*, 81–90. Los Alamitos, Calif.: IEEE Computer Society Press.

Brooks, F.P. Jr. 1987. No Silver Bullet: Essence and Accidents of Software Engineering. *Computer 20*: 10–9.

Brown, Alan W. 1996. Preface: Foundations for Component-Based Software Engineering. In *Component-Based Software Engineering: Selected Papers from the Software Engineering Institute*, vii–x. Los Alamitos, Calif.: IEEE Computer Society Press.

Brown, Alan W. and Kurt C. Wallnau. 1996. Engineering of Component-Based Systems. In *Component-Based Software Engineering: Selected Papers from the Software Engineering Institute*, 7–15. Los Alamitos, Calif.: IEEE Computer Society Press.

Clements, Paul C. 1996. From Subroutines to Subsystems: Component-Based Software Development. 3-6. *Component-Based Software Engineering: Selected Papers from the Software Engineering Institute.* Los Alamitos, CA: IEEE Computer Society Press.

IEEE. 1993. IEEE Recommended Practice on the Selection and Evaluation of CASE Tools. *IEEE Std. 1209–1992.* New York: Institute of Electrical and Electronics Engineers.

International Standards Organization/International Electrochemical Commission. 1991. Information Technology—Software Product Evaluation—Quality Characteristics and Guidelines for Their Use. Geneva, Switzerland.

Kontio, J. 1996. A Case Study in Applying a Systematic Method for COTS Selection. In *Proceedings of the 18th International Conference on Software Engineering in Berlin, Germany, March 25–30*, 201–209. Los Alamitos, Calif.: IEEE Computer Society Press.

Lettes, Judith A., and John Wilson. 1996. Army STARS Demonstration Project Experience Report. In *STARS-VC-A011/003/02*. Manassas, Va.: Loral Defense Systems-East.

Monfort, Lt. Col. Ralph D. 1996. Lessons Learned in the Development and Integration of a COTS-Based Satellite TT&C System. In *33rd Space Congress in Cocoa Beach, Florida. April 23–26.*

COTS-Based Development. http://www.isds.jpl.nasa.gov/cwo/cwo_23/handbook/Dsnswdhb.htm.

Create Mechanisms/Incentives for Reuse and COTS Use. http://bolero.gsfc.nasa.gov/c600/workshops/sswssp4b.htm.

PLAS. http://www.cards.com/plas.

Poston, R.M. and M.P. Sexton M.P. 1992. Evaluating and Selecting Testing Tools. *IEEE Software 9,* vol. 3: 33–42.

Portable, Reusable, Integrated Software Modules (PRISM) Program. http://www.cards.com/PRISM/prism_ov.html.

Air Force/STARS Demonstration Project Home Page. http://www.asset.com/stars/afdemo/home.html.

Thomas, I., and B. Nejmeh. 1992. Definitions of Tool Integration for Environments. *IEEE Software 9,* 3 (March 1992): 29–35.

Valetto, G., and G.E. Kaiser. 1995. Enveloping Sophisticated Tools into Computer-Aided Software Engineering Environments. In *Proceedings of 7th IEEE International Workshop on CASE in Toronto, Ontario, July 10–14,* 40–48. Los Alamitos, Calif.: IEEE Computer Society Press.

Vidger, M.R., W.M. Gentleman, and J. Dean. COTS Software Integration: State-of-the-Art. http://wwwsel.iit.nrc.ca/abstracts/NRC39198.abs.

Microsoft Corporation. 1998. Design Guides. Visual Basic 5.0 Documentation, Developer Products Book, MSDN Library. Microsoft Corporation.

Robertson, James, and Suzanne Robertson. 1997. Requirements: Made to Measure. Atlantic Systems Guild, Ltd.

___. 1996, 1998. *Volere Requirements Specification Template Version 6.0.* Atlantic Systems Guild, Ltd.

Robertson, Suzanne. 1996. An Early Start to Testing: How to Test Requirements. In *Conference Proceeding from Atlantic Systems Guild, Ltd.*

PMI Project Management Institute. http://www.pmi.org.

Figures and Tables

All figures and tables are courtesy of the author.

978-0-595-44433-5
0-595-44433-4